# ASIA–PACIFIC FINANCIAL INCLUSION FORUM 2021

## EMERGING PRIORITIES IN THE COVID-19 ERA

DECEMBER 2021

ADB

ASIAN DEVELOPMENT BANK

© 2021 Asian Development Bank
6 ADB Avenue, Mandaluyong City, 1550 Metro Manila, Philippines
Tel +63 2 8632 4444; Fax +63 2 8636 2444
www.adb.org

Some rights reserved. Published in 2021.

ISBN 978-92-9269-190-5 (print); 978-92-9269-191-2 (electronic); 978-92-9269-192-9 (ebook)
Publication Stock No. TCS210469-2
DOI: http://dx.doi.org/10.22617/TCS210469-2

Notes:
In this publication, "$" refers to United States dollars, unless otherwise stated.
ADB recognizes "China" as the People's Republic of China and "Hong Kong" as Hong Kong, China.

Cover design by Francis Joseph Manio.

# CONTENTS

# FIGURES, TABLES, BOXES, AND CASE STUDIES

# FOREWORD

Developing Asia has experienced remarkable economic growth and socioeconomic transformation over the past several decades. Nevertheless, the region continues to face enduring challenges of persistent poverty and increasing income inequality. The coronavirus disease (COVID-19) pandemic exacerbates these issues. Scarring inflicted by the pandemic on economies and human welfare threatens to reverse decades of hard-won gains in poverty alleviation and development across Asia. It hits those at the bottom of the economic pyramid the most, with women and other marginalized groups disproportionately affected. Yet every crisis presents opportunities. We need to embrace these by identifying effective policy responses—not only to support strong, sustained, and inclusive economic recovery, but also to rebuild smartly.

The pandemic has overturned many aspects of life, dramatically reshaping the way we work and live. It has also transformed financial systems worldwide toward considerably greater digitalization. Governments recognize the importance of financial inclusion, particularly digital financial inclusion, as a major driver of sustainable economic recovery. The Asia-Pacific Financial Inclusion Forum (APFIF), as a longstanding initiative of the Asia-Pacific Economic Cooperation (APEC) Finance Ministers' Process, is an important policy forum that enhances collective understanding of the importance of financial inclusion. Under the theme, "Emerging Priorities in the COVID-19 Era," this year's forum focused on the role fintech and innovative digital financial services can play in broadening financial inclusion and therefore realizing inclusive economic growth and resilience.

Based on the discussion, this publication provides valuable insights on the most effective ways financial inclusion strategies can be utilized to respond to the pandemic. This includes approaches for developing inclusive digital economies, supporting innovation, and improving the digital capabilities of institutions that serve the poor. The publication also examines emerging challenges and opportunities that result from an increasingly digitized world, such as the need to reconsider multiple dimensions of financial inclusion within the digital landscape. It is also imperative to develop innovative financing mechanisms to close digital infrastructure investment gaps and enhance efforts to ensure that digital finance services are both accessible and affordable to the poor.

This publication offers specific policy recommendations and steps for policy makers and regulators to consider to address these issues. It is my hope that these recommendations will provide useful guidance on how to harness digital financial services more effectively and ultimately lead us closer to the realization of an inclusive and prosperous region built upon a foundation of strong cooperation.

**Yasuyuki Sawada**
Chief Economist, March 2017–August 2021
Asian Development Bank

# ACKNOWLEDGMENTS

This publication was prepared by the Asian Development Bank (ADB), Regional Cooperation and Integration Division (ERCI) of the Economic Research and Regional Cooperation Department (ERCD) under the overall guidance and supervision of Cyn-Young Park, director, ERCI. The ADB Technical Assistance for Strengthening Regional Cooperation and Knowledge Sharing on the Application of Technology in Financial Services supported this project.

Shawn Hunter (consultant) and Peter Rosenkranz (economist, ERCI) are the main authors of this publication.

The publication greatly benefited from the discussions at the 11th annual Asia-Pacific Financial Inclusion Forum (APFIF) policy dialogue, which was held virtually on 25 May 2021, in collaboration with APEC Business Advisory Council (ABAC), Asian Development Bank Institute (ADBI), and the Foundation for Development Cooperation (FDC). The following forum speakers provided background material and reviewed specific sections of the publication: Lisette Cipriano (senior digital technology specialist [Financial Technology Services], ADB); Keyzom Ngodup Massally (head of Asia-Pacific, UN Better Than Cash Alliance); Douglas Arner (Kerry Holdings professor and RGC senior fellow in Digital Finance and Sustainable Development, University of Hong Kong); Sanjeev Kaushik (additional secretary, Financial Services Department, Ministry of Finance of India); Pieter Franken (director, The ASEAN Financial Innovation Network (AFIN)); Ulrich Volz (director of the Centre for Sustainable Finance, SOAS, University of London and senior research fellow, German Development Institute); Chuchi Fonacier (deputy governor, Bangko Sentral ng Pilipinas); Yunita Resmi Sari (executive director - head of SME Development and Consumer Protection Department, Bank Indonesia); and Nawaron Dejsuvan (assistant governor, Financial Institutions Policy Group, Bank of Thailand).

Helpful comments received from Julius Caesar Parrenas (senior advisor, Daiwa Institute of Research Ltd at Daiwa Securities Group); Stephen Taylor (executive director, FDC); and Peter Morgan (senior consulting economist, vice chair of Research, ADBI) are gratefully acknowledged.

The following forum speakers are also acknowledged for supporting both the forum and this publication: Bram Peters (program manager, Pacific Financial Inclusion Program, United Nations Capital Development Fund [UNCDF]); Yasuyuki Sawada (former chief economist and director general, ERCD, ADB); Tetsushi Sonobe (dean, ADBI); and Hiroshi Nakaso (Chair, ABAC Advisory Group on APEC Financial System Capacity Building).

ADBI staff who supported the organization and conduct of the forum include Pitchaya Sirivunnabood (capacity building and training economist), Kayo Tsuchiya (program coordinator), and Alexander Boden (capacity building and training associate).

An earlier version of the publication has been submitted to APEC Finance Ministers in October 2021.

Peter Rosenkranz and Paulo Rodelio Halili (senior economics officer, ERCI, ADB) coordinated the production of this publication, with support from Marilyn Parra (senior operations assistant, ERCI, ADB).

James Unwin edited the manuscript, Francis Joseph Manio created the cover design, and Jennifer Flint implemented the typesetting and layout. Layla Yasmin Tanjutco-Amar proofread the publication, while Ma. Cecilia Abellar handled the page proof checking, and Michael Cortes provided additional illustrations. The Printing Services Unit of ADB's Corporate Services Department and the Publishing Team of the Department of Communications supported printing and publishing.

# ABBREVIATIONS

| | | |
|---|---|---|
| ABAC | – | APEC Business Advisory Council |
| ADB | – | Asian Development Bank |
| APEC | – | Asia-Pacific Economic Cooperation |
| APFIF | – | Asia-Pacific Financial Inclusion Forum |
| API | – | application program interface |
| APIX | – | Application Program Interface Exchange |
| ASEAN | – | Association of Southeast Asian Nations |
| BSP | – | Bangko Sentral ng Pilipinas |
| COVID-19 | – | coronavirus disease |
| eKYC | – | electronic know your customer |
| ESCAP | – | United Nations Economic and Social Commission for Asia and the Pacific |
| GDCF | – | gross domestic capital formation |
| GDP | – | gross domestic product |
| ICT | – | information and communication technology |
| ID | – | identification |
| IMF | – | International Monetary Fund |
| MSMEs | – | micro, small, and medium-sized enterprises |
| NIE | – | newly industrialized economy |

# EXECUTIVE SUMMARY

The coronavirus disease (COVID-19) pandemic increased the importance of access to financial services, given their role in supporting economic recovery and resilience. In response, the Asian Development Bank (ADB) and its partners in the Asia-Pacific Financial Inclusion Forum (APFIF) have identified financial inclusion priorities and recommendations for governments to improve their support for the region's most vulnerable populations and stimulate economic recovery. The APFIF is a policy initiative of the Asia-Pacific Economic Cooperation (APEC) Finance Ministers' Process. It was proposed by the APEC Business Advisory Council (ABAC) to identify actions policy makers and regulators can take to put financial services within the reach of the underserved.

## Digital Transformation during the COVID-19 Pandemic

In response to the pandemic, many governments have prioritized the digital economy to improve innovation and inclusion. Acceleration of digital transformation, including within the finance sector, has been unprecedented as a result. In relation to financial inclusion, many governments support the development of digital payments systems and expansion of bank deposits to facilitate rapid and efficient cash transfers to those in need and to enable continued economic activity during lockdowns and social distancing. However, as digital transformation gathers pace, the growing digital divide is generating new inequality challenges.

Many governments, especially in developing economies with less-developed capital markets continue to face significant financing gaps for digital infrastructure development. Closing the gaps and enabling safe, reliable, and affordable digital infrastructure is also critical to achieving digital financial inclusion.

### Facilitating Recovery and Resilience through Financial Inclusion

The pandemic has had significant economic impact, especially on vulnerable and disadvantaged groups, including informal workers, the poor, and women. With the road to economic recovery likely to be long and challenging, innovative approaches to financial inclusion are needed to rebuild livelihoods and increase resilience among the poorest and most vulnerable.

While digital finance can be important for facilitating recovery and resilience, questions remain about its viability to support the poorest segments of the region's population, who often lack necessary skills or access to adequate infrastructure. Traditionally, microfinance providers have played a pivotal role in providing financial services to those at the base of the economy, including micro, small, and medium-sized enterprises. Leveraging their reach and trust with clients, microfinance providers have the opportunity to adopt digital technology in ways that can bring the benefits of the digital economy to clients, particularly during the pandemic.

When addressing financial market infrastructure gaps, priorities should focus on providing immediate relief through digital social payments and generating income to support growth and build resilience against future shocks. Digital payments channels, digital identification, and effective capture and usage of data, achieve these outcomes by enabling direct, targeted, and efficient economic stimulus.

The COVID-19 pandemic has highlighted the advantages of a well-developed digital economy for digital financial services to respond more effectively to the crisis. However, for digital technology to have meaningful impact on the region's most vulnerable populations, greater innovation is also needed to develop new approaches and business models. Governments can support this by including finance sector innovation in their pandemic recovery strategies, including development of an ecosystem that supports digital transformation and establishing a regulatory environment for safe fintech innovation.

## Emerging Financial Inclusion Challenges and Opportunities in a World Disrupted by COVID-19

As technology developments continue to accelerate in response to the COVID-19 pandemic, governments need to consider how these developments are now shaping the post-pandemic world. Expansion of digital services during the pandemic will increase pressure on policy makers and regulators to ensure it leads to greater inclusion and prosperity, including by developing safe and reliable fintech markets and supporting other opportunities to accelerate progress.

The pandemic continues to speed up the pace of technology and fintech developments, including innovative digital products and services now entering the market. While studies have shown financial inclusion has positive impact on aspects such as poverty, income inequality, women's empowerment, and entrepreneurship, the financial inclusion landscape is changing rapidly with the acceleration of technology in financial markets. To ensure that financial inclusion has the greatest impact on socioeconomic outcomes, governments need to ensure their strategies continue to meet the challenges of an increasingly digital world.

The fintech sector continues to expand, partly due to COVID-19, yet many financial institutions are still unable to serve all their customers digitally; particularly those at the lower income ends of the market. Furthermore, very few fintechs or traditional financial institutions are focused on providing digital services to people on low incomes because of persistent challenges such as high illiteracy, reliance on cash, lack of digital financial literacy, or limited access to digital infrastructure. As the usability of technology improves, governments can support cooperation between fintechs and financial institutions to enable more people on low incomes to receive, and benefit from, digital services.

Given the persistent financing gaps for digital infrastructure development, emerging fintech models such as asset tokenization, blockchain-based project bonds, or crowdfunding can also provide innovative solutions for raising capital.

## Recommendations for Policy Makers and Regulators

(i)    *Support the capacity of microfinance providers to adopt digital technology to drive financial inclusion and bring the benefits of the digital economy to their clients by*

- promoting and ensuring equitable access to digital infrastructure among microfinance providers including support for interoperable payment systems to close the digital divide for all participants in the ecosystem and expanding investment in digital infrastructure,

- developing and promoting a fully functioning digital identity system to help microfinance providers carry out due diligence requirements and enable greater participation in the digital economy, and

- developing enabling policy and enhancing regulation for new technologies in close coordination with other government agencies that also support innovation and technology.

(ii)    *Prioritize investments in open digital ecosystems that accelerate digitization of payments leading to inclusive recovery, resilience, and financial inclusion by*

- supporting the development of responsible digital ecosystems through investments in platform design, architecture, and technical support with the aim of reducing systemic exclusion of the most vulnerable from a large range of financial services;

- facilitating the creation and implementation of good governance to address new risks and the amplification of existing risks (i.e., potential for increased fraud), arising from increased digital financial transfers; and

- supporting growth of a vibrant technology community, including open-source technology start-ups and civil-society stakeholders as stewards of user experiences.

(iii)    *Support innovation as part of COVID-19 recovery strategies by*

- building the infrastructure of digital finance with a focus on digital access (i.e., mobile or internet) for as much of the population as possible and achieving the needed combination of sovereign digital identification, simplified account opening, and systems to enable effective data collection and usage;

- designing regulatory approaches that are risk-based, tiered, and proportional— so that as risk increases, so too does regulation and supervision; and

- providing support for the wider data ecosystem including the development of a framework for data collection and use, and to enable data to support development while minimizing associated risks.

(iv)    *Reassess financial inclusion strategies to consider the growing use of digital financial services by*

- building a digital transformation roadmap to achieve scale by facilitating implementation of consistent cooperation among a wider set of stakeholders;

- considering new dimensions of financial inclusion such as fintech infrastructure and financial development, which are increasingly viewed as key contributors to financial inclusion;

- recognizing that the impact of financial inclusion varies depending on the economy's state of development to establish more effective policies that account for how dimensions of financial inclusion have different impacts depending on the income levels of economies; and

- prioritizing financial inclusion policies that will have a greater effect on socioeconomic outcomes including ensuring adequate attention is paid to demand-side factors such as digital finance literacy programs to improve trust and confidence in the digital finance ecosystem and drive greater usage and impact.

(v)    *Take steps to promote greater stakeholder cooperation to progress digital financial inclusion at the base of the economy by*

- reimagining regulatory technology risk management frameworks to align more effectively with contemporary technology and promoting a more efficient de-risking by bringing together multiple fintechs to support rapid digital product prototyping;

- fast-tracking regulatory licensing for microfinance providers to go digital by leveraging existing frameworks rather than treating each digital journey as a standalone case and providing standard, open application program interfaces (APIs) to streamline reporting requirements; and

- establishing legislation with clear timelines for fully open banking APIs for domestic incumbent players to support integration and connectivity within the financial ecosystem, giving equal treatment to smaller microfinance providers and local and/or global fintechs and speeding up digitalization.

**(vi)    *Explore the potential of innovative fintech financing mechanisms for digital infrastructure development needs by***

- identifying and investing in key digital systems to harness innovative fintech solutions for raising investment capital such as crowdfunding platforms, digital bonds using mobile banking platforms, or the tokenization of debt and/or equity instruments;

- nurturing talent to enhance internal capabilities such as placement of technology experts within central banks or government ministries and establishing a dedicated technology innovation group or expert network to provide functions such as identifying innovative models and use cases, facilitating public–private collaboration or coordination with international partners; and

- exploring innovative fintech solutions to mobilize domestic savings by identifying fintech solutions that may be most effective, and creating adequate regulatory frameworks that allow development of promising fintech solutions while safeguarding financial stability and consumer protection.

# 1. INTRODUCTION

The Asia-Pacific Financial Inclusion Forum (APFIF) is an Asia-Pacific Economic Cooperation (APEC) initiative to help expand the benefits of useful, affordable, and sustainable financial products and services to those at the base of the economy.[1] It plays an important role, both in the annual APEC process and in supporting broader regional cooperation efforts. Each year the initiative brings together senior government officials, industry leaders, and development experts to explore the trends, opportunities, and challenges associated with financial inclusion and to identify the most viable and practical solutions to accelerate progress. After more than a decade, APFIF has established itself among policy makers and regulators as a preeminent platform for building capacity across Asia and the Pacific.

*"The Asia-Pacific Financial Inclusion Forum has been the most enduring initiative under the APEC Finance Ministers' Process, and one of the most successful."* Hiroshi Nakaso, Chair, ABAC Advisory Group on APEC Financial System Capacity Building

In recent years, APFIF has increased its focus on the challenges and opportunities presented by the digital revolution and the role of digital financial services in advancing financial inclusion. This has become of greater importance as governments increasingly concentrate on digitalization and inclusion as major pillars of economic recovery strategies in response to the coronavirus disease (COVID-19) pandemic.[2] The themes of digitalization and inclusion also feature in APEC's Putrajaya Vision 2040, which promotes specific economic drivers to increase prosperity, and among the priorities of APEC's Host Economy for 2021, New Zealand, which has adopted the theme *"Join. Work. Grow. Together. Haumi ē, Hui ē, Tāiki ē."* This is a call for APEC economies to pursue recovery measures promoting inclusion, sustainability, and digital innovation.

The APFIF initiative, under the APEC Finance Ministers' Process, stands to play a very important role in exploring new challenges associated with the growing digital divide and helping ensure digital economies create new economic opportunities for marginalized segments of the population, including microenterprises, women, or other disadvantaged groups. To support this, a policy dialogue involving senior government officials from the region and industry experts was convened through APFIF on 25 May 2021. Under the theme *"Emerging Priorities in the COVID-19 Era,"* the dialogue examined the role of financial

---

[1]   The term "base of the economy" refers to the poorest socioeconomic segment, including individuals, households, and the microenterprises they operate.

[2]   The term "digitization" refers to the conversion of data or processes to a digital form while "digitalization" refers to the transformation of an organization's processes to leverage digital technologies.

inclusion in supporting economic recovery and how the recent growth of the digital economy is creating new challenges and opportunities. Specific topics included:

(i)     digital transformation during the COVID-19 pandemic,
(ii)    facilitating recovery and resilience through financial inclusion, and
(iii)   emerging financial inclusion challenges and opportunities in a world disrupted by COVID-19.

This publication provides an overview of each topic and includes the specific recommendations for policy makers and regulators identified and developed through the Policy Dialogue. The recommendations in this publication are not intended to cover every major issue associated with those topics, but rather have been formulated to align with the priorities of APEC in 2021 and their perceived impact on the poorest and most vulnerable populations.

The Asian Development Bank (ADB) leads the APFIF initiative with support provided by the Foundation for Development Cooperation (FDC) and the Asian Development Bank Institute. It is one of three platforms for collaboration among the public and private sectors and multilateral institutions whose general oversight is entrusted to APEC Business Advisory Council.[3]

---

[3]    The other two are the Asia-Pacific Financial Forum (APFF), established in 2013, and the Asia-Pacific Infrastructure Partnership, established in 2011.

# 2. DIGITAL TRANSFORMATION DURING THE COVID-19 PANDEMIC

Rapid development and adoption of digital technologies in recent years has helped shape economic growth across Asia and the Pacific. With strong support from many governments and development practitioners in the region, the appeal of utilizing technology to advance sustainable development and inclusive economic growth has led to significant advances in the region's digital economy. This includes strengthening information and communication technology (ICT) infrastructure and the provision of digital services, as well as additional support mechanisms such as digital skill development programs and cybersecurity policies.

The rate of digitalization across the world has increased exponentially since the COVID-19 pandemic began. As businesses sought ways to facilitate services remotely during lockdowns and the implementation of social distancing measures, the need for new operating models pushed many institutions to adopt digital technologies and enable various remote functionalities. This phenomenon was highlighted by Microsoft's CEO, Satya Nadella, who stated during a quarterly earnings call in April 2020 that *"we've seen two years of digital transformation in two months"* (Spataro 2020). Such unprecedented growth was highlighted by McKinsey and Company, which found that responses to COVID-19 accelerated the adoption of digital technologies globally by several years (Figures 1 and 2).

## Figure 1: Average Share of Customer Interactions That Are Digital (%)

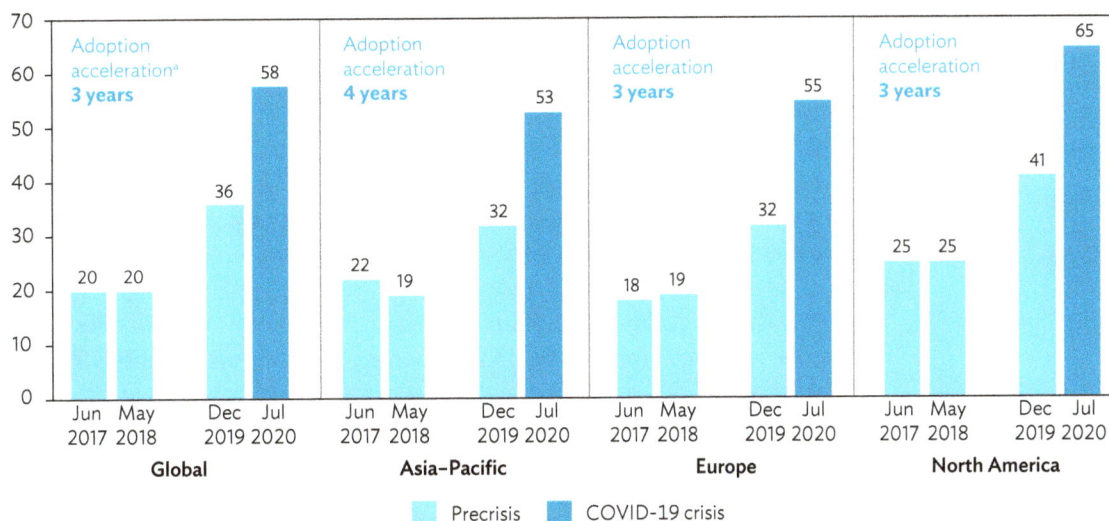

[a] Years ahead of the average rate of adoption from 2017 to 2019.

Source: *McKinsey and Company*. 2020. How COVID-19 Has Pushed Companies Over the Technology Tipping Point—and Transformed Business Forever. https://www.mckinsey.com/business-functions/strategy-and-corporate-finance/our-insights/how-covid-19-has-pushed-companies-over-the-technology-tipping-point-and-transformed-business-forever (accessed 20 February 2021).

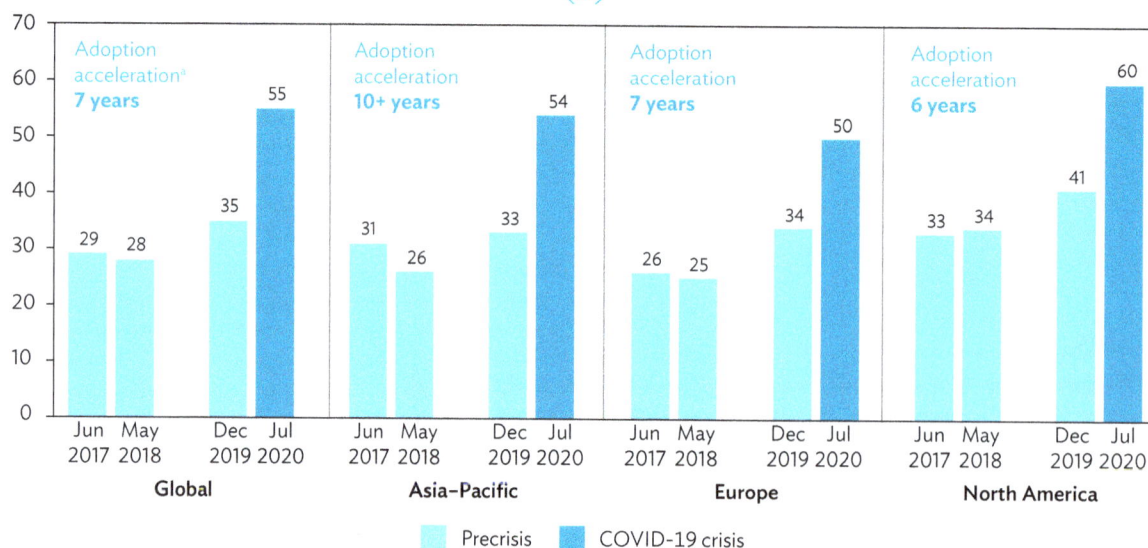

**Figure 2: Average Share of Products and/or Services That Are Partially or Fully Digitized (%)**

[a] Years ahead of the average rate of adoption from 2017 to 2019.

Source: *McKinsey and Company*. 2020. How COVID-19 Has Pushed Companies Over the Technology Tipping Point— and Transformed Business Forever. https://www.mckinsey.com/business-functions/strategy-and-corporate-finance/ our-insights/how-covid-19-has-pushed-companies-over-the-technology-tipping-point-and-transformed-business-forever (accessed 20 February 2021).

*"COVID-19 has accelerated the scale and reach of digitization in finance throughout Asia-Pacific, catalyzing G2P payments with 166 governments launching 429 cash transfer programs and expanding the number of G2P payments by 1.1 billion people in 2020."* Stephen Taylor, Executive Director, The Foundation for Development Cooperation

The pace of digital transformation in Asia and the Pacific has increased with the pandemic driving more consumers toward online platforms for social and economic activities. This has led to significant demand on existing digital infrastructure as well as unprecedented growth opportunities for "digital-ready" businesses. For example, during the early stages of the pandemic, online data traffic in the Republic of Korea increased by 13% while a single operator in Japan reported that data traffic increased by as much 40% (GSMA 2020). In the Philippines, GCash, a major mobile wallet company, experienced a 700% year-on-year increase in transaction volume in a single month and doubled its registered users in the first half of 2020 (ADB 2021a). This acceleration of digital transformation in Asia and the Pacific has not only presented important opportunities for economic activity to continue throughout the crisis, but is also creating new ones to integrate with the global economy and support broader growth and recovery (ADB 2021a).

The push to digitalize in an effort to mitigate the economic fallout of the pandemic has gained some prominence in the responses of many governments. Often with the support of development practitioners, governments have, in varying degrees, increased efforts to introduce technology solutions to respond to the needs of citizens during the crisis and to keep their economies functioning. Just as the People's Republic of China expedited the launch of digital payments and e-commerce during the severe acute respiratory syndrome (SARS) epidemic in 2003 (Xiao and Chorzempa 2020), many governments have taken action to accelerate the development or adoption of e-services such as digital information-sharing platforms, e-commerce, digital government-to-person (G2P) social protection transfers or digital payments systems (Benni 2021). For example, the World Bank in May 2020 reported that at least 11 developing economies had suspended or reduced mobile money transaction fees and issued guidelines to encourage the use of mobile payments (Begazo 2020).

Government priorities for digitalization have varied across economies in accordance with local social, political, and economic factors. In emerging and low-income economies, increasing the capabilities for rapid disbursement of cash relief to citizens has been common. Due to developing economies having large informal sectors, labor market policies aimed at protecting jobs during the pandemic have been difficult to implement. As such, many have instead prioritized cash transfers to support households and small businesses, and in several cases, governments have leveraged mobile technology to facilitate payments (Davidovic et al. 2020). For example,

### Case Study 1: Government-led Digitalization in Thailand

The Government of Thailand has identified digital technology as a key driver to accelerate financial inclusion and support economic resilience and recovery during the coronavirus disease pandemic. A significant milestone in this strategy was reached following the successful launch of the PromptPay project that was launched in 2017 and established an economy-wide service for individuals and businesses to receive and transfer funds electronically. The digital services enabled through the PromptPay project have significantly increased in their value to customers as a result of the pandemic and the need for more remote transactions.

In 2021, PromptPay was expanded through a digital payment linkage with Singapore's Paynow platform, enabling customers of participating banks to transfer funds between the two economies with ease. This important milestone, the first of its kind globally, was a product of government collaboration under the ASEAN Payment Connectivity Scheme that was launched to facilitate cheaper, faster, more inclusive, and transparent cross-border transactions in the region (Banchongduang 2021).

Building upon the success of the PromptPay project, the central bank, the Bank of Thailand, has initiated two new programs that aim to further utilize technology to expand the reach of formal financial services to unbanked or underserved communities.

**Digital Personal Loan Program**. Through this program, the government has allowed banks and nonbank financial institutions that are already granting personal loans to begin offering new digital loans to underserved communities. By using technology to gather alternative data sources such as bill payments or online shopping transactions, the banks can evaluate a customer's ability to pay more effectively. By doing so, the government hopes more banks can provide formal financial services to low-income customers and reduce the need to resort to loans sharks. As a result, over 100,000 small new loans (i.e., about $100 per person) were distributed to underserved individuals in the first few months of 2021. This support has been important to many people and micro, small, and medium-sized enterprises in Thailand who faced financial stress because of economic impacts of the pandemic.

**Digital Factoring Ecosystem Development Project**. In collaboration with public and private organizations, this program aims to support small firms as crucial elements of larger supply chains. Traditionally, these have significant difficulty in accessing funding from formal financial institutions. The program aims to address this by developing a new ecosystem based on a digital solution, including necessary infrastructure, which will facilitate end-to-end factoring. To support this, the Bank of Thailand and stakeholders have developed a digital invoice standard for factoring which enables invoice data to be processed digitally and so reduces the risk of fraud.

ASEAN = Association of Southeast Asian Nations.

Source: N. Dejsuvan. 2021. Remarks at the 2021 Asia-Pacific Financial Inclusion Forum. 25 May.

*"We strongly believe that digital transformation accelerates and plays an important role in the integration of economic development and financial inclusion."* Yunita Resmi Sari, Executive Director, Head of SME Development and Consumer Protection Department, Bank Indonesia

in March 2020, the Government of Thailand initiated a major digital cash transfer program for 3 million informal workers. This program utilized several channels to transfer B5,000 in handouts to individuals, including the government-initiated PromptPay digital platform (Bangkok Post 2020). Additional features of Thailand's PromptPay initiative are outlined in Case Study 1 below.

The pandemic has illustrated how economies that have already invested in developing a strong digital infrastructure and have actively encouraged the adoption of digital services are more capable of ensuring continued access to digital services, including rapid deployment of G2P payments that can more easily reach the informal sector (Rutkowski et al. 2020).

## Digitalization for Pandemic Recovery

While the pandemic may have increased interest in digitalization, the use of technology as a key driver of economic growth has been at the forefront of development agendas and strategies for several years. Many governments in the region and development institutions, including ADB, the United Nations, and the World Bank, have increasingly promoted the benefits of digital transformation among sectors including health, agriculture, finance, energy, or education. Digitalization strategies have also been integrated into international policy forums, such as APEC and the Group of 20, which frequently promote the need for greater cross-border collaboration on technology-related issues such as digitally enabled international trade or facilitating cross-border data flows.

Following the recent spike in global efforts to accelerate digitalization to mitigate the immediate impacts of the pandemic, many governments and development stakeholders are now shifting their focus toward effective and sustainable post-pandemic recovery. Within this focus, digitalization continues to be featured heavily within strategies to accelerate the repair of damaged economies. For example, in late 2020 the European Union announced a €1.8 trillion stimulus package to build "a greener, more digital and more resilient Europe" (European Commission 2020) with 20% of the planned investment earmarked for digital matters such as connectivity, skills, digital public services, and artificial intelligence (CEPIS 2020). APEC leaders have also cited digital transformation as a key aspect of post-COVID-19 recovery and included "Innovation and Digitalization" as one of the core pillars of the APEC Putrajaya Vision 2040, which sets out principles and guidance for economies to achieve "an open, dynamic resilient and peaceful Asia-Pacific community by 2040, for the prosperity of all our people and future generations" (APEC 2021). By prioritizing digital transformation, particularly expanding digital infrastructure, and supporting the digitalization of micro, small, and medium-sized enterprises (MSMEs), governments can leverage the momentum of the recent growth and adoption of digital services to accelerate economic recovery.

The potential gains from prioritizing digital transformation are significant. For example, ADB has forecasted that a 20% increase in the size of Asia's digital sector could increase trade revenue by as much as $1 trillion and create as many as

65 million jobs per year (ADB 2021a). A study in India concluded that progressing the digitalization of MSMEs could be a major contributor to post-pandemic economic recovery by adding as much as $216 billion gross domestic product (GDP) by 2024 (Dash 2020). This potential to drive growth and recovery by enhancing MSME participation in the digital economy is especially significant in Asia with MSMEs in member states of the Association of Southeast Asian Nations (ASEAN), accounting for 95% to 99% of all businesses, more than half of total employment, and contributing as much as 53% to their respective economies (Paine 2021). As the backbone of economies, supporting the digitalization of MSMEs and enabling new ways for them to conduct business online, reduce costs, and reach new markets can be a major driver of economic growth while supporting the livelihoods and well-being of millions of people on low incomes.

## Exacerbating the Digital Divide

Besides recognizing the potential for digitization to help economic recovery and foster greater resilience post-pandemic, many governments and development stakeholders also promote this new wave of digital transformation as an opportunity to rebuild economies in ways that result in greater sustainability and inclusiveness, especially for marginalized groups including women, youth, and the elderly. Such resolve was demonstrated in the APEC 2020 Leaders' Declaration, which called for commitments to achieve "strong, balanced, inclusive, sustainable, innovative and secure" economic recovery from the pandemic, with a strong focus on inclusive economic participation through digital economy and technology (APEC 2020).

Increasing efforts to achieve inclusiveness, as well as digital inclusion, could have a significant impact for millions of people, especially in Asia and the Pacific, which is often characterized by significant inequality. In 2018, prior to the pandemic, the United Nations Economic and Social Commission for Asia and the Pacific (ESCAP) reported a widening of disparities in income and wealth generation, uneven access to opportunities and basic services, and that inequality was leading to environmental degradation and disasters impacting the poorest (ESCAP 2018). More recent research by the International Monetary Fund (IMF) found the COVID-19 pandemic has worsened inequality, particularly income inequality, with women and youth impacted most severely (Jurzyk et al. 2020).

The IMF research also concluded that government efforts to prioritize digitalization in economic recovery strategies could also add new risks to inequality. For example, traditional jobs lost during the pandemic might be replaced by jobs with greater digital integration, and require different skill sets. In these cases, those at the base of the economy, with more limited digital skills, would suffer most.

Digital inclusion refers to the ability of individuals or businesses to reap the benefits of the digital economy, including being online and using technology, in ways that improve well-being. For those at the base of the economy, particularly those in developing or low-income economies, the opportunities to leverage digital tools or services to support their lives or enterprise are often limited or nonexistent (Box 1).

---

### Box 1: Critical Gaps in the Digital Divide Common in Low-Income Economies

Less than **10%** of households are fixed broadband subscribers

Over **30%** of populations lack access to 4G mobile connectivity

The cost of monthly broadband subscription is **12%** of gross national income, far higher than the United Nations target of 2% by 2025

Smartphone ownership is only **30%-60%**, and PC ownership is only **21%**

Only **32%** of the population has basic digital skills

Source: Adapted from World Economic Forum. 2020. *Accelerating Digital Inclusion in the New Normal*. Geneva. http://www3.weforum.org/docs/WEF_Accelerating_Digital_Inclusion_in_the_New_Normal_Report_2020.pdf (accessed 23 February 2021).

---

Addressing this is a significant challenge requiring consideration of many factors, including the availability of technology (computers, mobile phones, etc.), suitable ICT infrastructure to enable connectivity (such as phone and internet networks), and user capability (digital skills, basic literacy, and the like). All of this must be affordable to poor households, many on incomes of less than $2 a day.

As governments, businesses, and development practitioners increase their focus on promoting digital transformation as a response to the economic crisis created by COVID-19, new inequality challenges are emerging in the form of the growing digital divide. While the full scale of the pandemic impact and digital responses to mitigate economic damage will likely not be known for some time, it has quickly become clear in many economies that the digitization of essential services, including health care, finance, and education, can lead to a situation where access to, and capability to use, technology shifts from an advantage to a necessity. In other words, addressing heightened exposure to the divide between those with the resources to take advantage of digital transformation, and those without is critical to the overall performance of the digital economy, its potential to accelerate recovery, and impact on the well-being of people at the base of the economy.

# 3. FACILITATING RECOVERY AND RESILIENCE THROUGH FINANCIAL INCLUSION

The economic impact of the COVID-19 pandemic has been significant. In late 2020, the IMF estimated that the global economy had shrunk by 4.4%—the worst decline since the Great Depression in the 1930s (Gopinath 2020). In developing Asia, the economy shrunk by 0.2%, with South Asia the hardest hit (ADB 2021b). Those at the base of the economy, many of whom operate in the informal sector and lack access to public or private safety nets, have been particularly vulnerable to the impact of this global economic fallout. The IMF further estimated that the economic impact of the pandemic could push as many as 90 million people into extreme poverty, representing a major reversal of steady poverty alleviation gains over the last 20 years (Figure 3).[4] With the pandemic stifling growth potential for many economies, recovery is expected to be slow. For example, disruptions to education caused by COVID-19 will significantly impact future productivity and economic growth potential with future earning losses estimated to be as much as $1.25 trillion for developing Asia (ADB 2021b). Despite projections that many economies will return to growth in 2021, the immediate decline in poverty is expected to be small with an overall increase because the crisis is expected to be long-lasting (World Bank 2020a and Kharas 2020).

*"While economic growth across developing Asia has shown promising signs of revival since the start of the crisis, resurgent outbreaks of COVID-19, coupled with vaccination rollout challenges, shows that the threat is far from over."* Yasuyuki Sawada, former Chief Economist and Director General, Economic Research and Regional Cooperation Department, Asian Development Bank

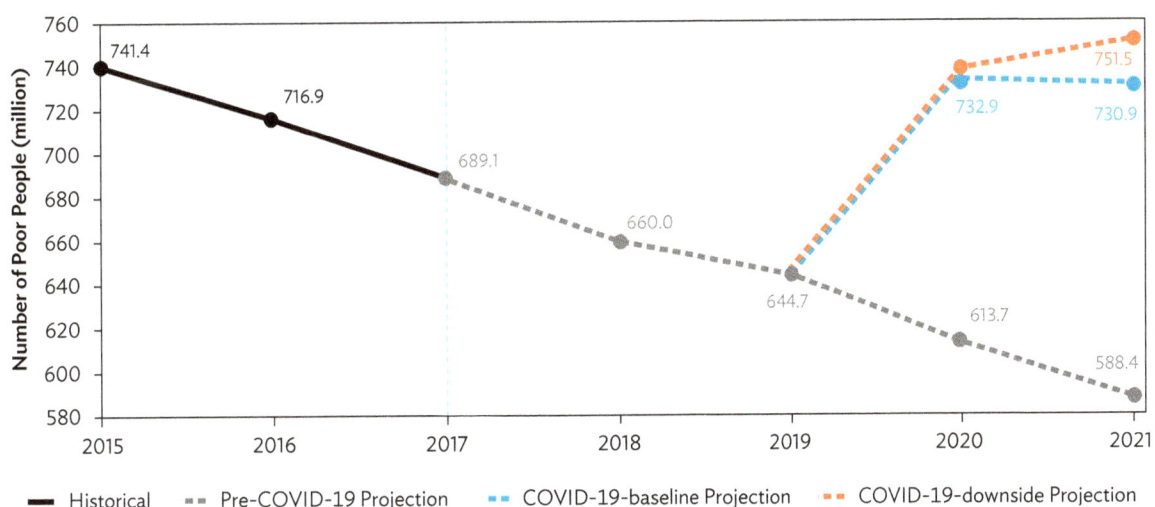

Figure 3: Nowcast of Extreme Poverty (Global), 2015–2021

Source: C. Lakner et al. 2021. Updated Estimates of the Impact of COVID-19 on Global Poverty: Looking Back at 2020 and the Outlook for 2021. *World Bank Blog*. 11 January. https://blogs.worldbank.org/opendata/updated-estimates-impact-covid-19-global-poverty-looking-back-2020-and-outlook-2021 (accessed 28 February 2021).

[4] According to the World Bank, extreme poverty is measured as the number of people living on less than $1.90 per day. https://www.worldbank.org/en/topic/measuringpoverty#1

*"COVID-19 has boosted the public awareness of the true social values of financial technology and the necessity of financial inclusion."* Tetsushi Sonobe, Dean, Asian Development Bank Institute

With the road to recovery likely to be long and challenging, especially for developing economies, it is important that governments develop recovery strategies around priorities that will produce the most effective results. While the specifics will differ between economies, considering their own domestic situation including current infrastructure development, geography, political, or other social dynamics, and so on, every economy should aim to ensure that strategies acknowledge the unique challenges faced by those on low or no income and strive to introduce solutions that foster inclusive recovery. This recognition is particularly important for strategies focusing on developing the digital economy, as there remain significant barriers for the base of the economy to engage effectively with digital technology, given its limited utility to the poor, weak business case for providers, and underdeveloped public infrastructure or supervision (Hunter and Taylor 2020).

Accelerating financial inclusion can be an important component of economic recovery strategies. However, to utilize financial inclusion as an effective driver of increased well-being and prosperity for people at the base of the economy, it needs to be focused on building resilience and capturing opportunities (Hernandez 2020). The COVID-19 pandemic has heightened the importance of this paradigm shift and highlighted the role financial inclusion plays in providing direct benefits to the poor and vulnerable.

This section of the publication examines the role of policy makers and regulators in achieving financial inclusion that supports economic recovery by adopting approaches that focus on building inclusive digital economies through strengthening the capacity of financial service providers and clients, developing financial market infrastructure most crucial for economic recovery and resilience, and accelerating innovation to tackle new and persistent challenges.

## Building Inclusive Digital Economies for Financial Inclusion

The COVID-19 pandemic has had a significant impact on global fintech markets and the provision of digital financial services. The disruptions caused by lockdown measures have created unprecedented demand in developing economies for digitally enabled financial products and services ranging from remittances, savings, insurance, or access to capital. The increase in demand was highlighted in a joint study by the World Bank, the World Economic Forum, and the Cambridge Centre for Alternative Finance at the University of Cambridge's Judge Business School. The study found that in developing economies, digital financial services (except for lending) saw strong growth during the pandemic (World Bank 2020b). As examples, in 2020, the mobile wallet GCash in the Philippines saw a 254% year-on-year growth in transactions (Gaylican 2021) while Bank Indonesia reported 38.62% growth in electronic money transfers (Crisanto 2021). Such expansion has undoubtedly helped to progress financial inclusion, however, as governments also turn their focus toward digitalization as a core element of economic recovery strategies, it is important to recognize the growing digital divide and the risk that this transformation might further exclude those at the base of the economy.

The benefits of introducing digital financial services to the poor, such as lower costs, instantaneous transactions, convenience, and greater control, are well-known. Digital financial services are also believed to have a wider impact, with research finding a positive association between digital financial inclusion, GDP growth, and closing gender gaps (Sahay et al. 2020). However, as the fintech market and provision of digital financial services continue to grow, evidence show that it is predominantly benefiting the underbanked but is less successful in engaging the unbanked (Hunter and Taylor 2020 and Bull 2020).

In developing and emerging economies, many poor and vulnerable groups rely on microfinance providers (i.e., microfinance institutions, cooperatives, nongovernment organizations, savings cooperatives, or self-help groups) to access financial products and services for basic needs such as savings, receiving and sending payments, or borrowing. As the COVID-19 crisis unfolded, many institutions that could not create virtual operations came under significant strain, struggling with liquidity stress, inability to collect loans, and branch closures through lockdowns. Understanding that microfinance firms provide important services to the poorest and most vulnerable communities, including through high-touch business models and a traditional focus on achieving positive social outcomes, is critical to developing solutions that will enable the development of digital finance infrastructure and services that foster inclusiveness.

As Bull (2020) pointed out, there are probably limits to how well fintech models can serve low-income clients due to lack of access and acceptance of digital technology among the poorest and most vulnerable. However, as fintechs continue to take more market share, microfinance providers will find it increasingly difficult to achieve scale, threatening the ability of many to survive. Until digital finance can live up to its full promise (i.e., providing financial products and services to the base of the economy responsibly and sustainably), traditional microfinance providers will continue to play an important role, especially for vulnerable women. The recent acceleration of digitalization is drawing attention to the shortfalls of fintech models with millions of poor households and MSMEs unable to access digital financial services due to persistent challenges such as underdeveloped ICT infrastructure, lack of digital skills and financial literacy, or the cost barriers to enabling access to technology.

An important reason for the success of many microfinance providers in selling services to the base of the economy has been their use of face-to-face interaction, or high-touch business models.[5] This approach is particularly important when operating in low-income communities where people often lack basic literacy or enterprise development skills to help them utilize financial products or services effectively. The high-touch business models create opportunities for service providers to directly develop their clients' capacity while also establishing relationships of trust. Many fintechs are incapable of mirroring these business advantages, which underscores the importance of microfinance providers being able to continue serving the base of the economy effectively.[6]

*"The introduction of technology and digital solutions provides a lot of new opportunities for financial inclusion; however, it is not a silver bullet, particularly since many of the business models for these solutions thrive on volume and the addressable markets are often quite limited, which is especially true for the Pacific."* Bram Peters, Program Manager – Pacific Financial Inclusion Program, United Nations Capital Development Fund (UNCDF)

*"In order to maintain relevance in an increasingly digital world, microfinance providers will need to adopt technology to retain resiliency, maintain their ability to provide services to customers, remain competitive and achieve scale."* Lisette Cipriano, Senior Digital Technology Specialist (Financial Technology Services), Asian Development Bank

---

[5]  High-touch business models refer to businesses that engage with customers through human interaction (e.g., field officers of a microfinance provider) as opposed to transacting through digital technology.

[6]  For more information about the unique advantages of traditional microfinance providers in providing services to the base of the economy, refer to the report produced by APFIF in 2020: *Enabling Shared Prosperity Through Inclusive Finance: Leaving No One Behind in an Age of Disruption.*

To address this challenge, rather than focusing on expanding the reach of fintechs with the hope that they may eventually be capable of serving poor and vulnerable groups effectively, efforts could be made to support partnerships that strengthen the technology capabilities of traditional microfinance providers and in turn bring the benefits of the digital economy to clients. To address this, ADB has initiated several pilot programs to enhance the digital capabilities of microfinance providers and establish best practices to support governments and practitioners. Examples of pilot programs are discussed in Case Study 2.

## Case Study 2: Supporting Digital Transformation of Microfinance Providers

Digital transformation for microfinance providers can be a very difficult and complex journey. As part of its ongoing commitment to support the microfinance industry, the Asian Development Bank (ADB) has developed several digitization initiatives across the region. These pilots aim to provide operational efficiencies and give pilot participants digital tools to help them achieve their financial inclusion goals. Throughout implementation, the support of financial regulators has been a key to success.

### Georgia: Digitization for Onboarding New Clients
The ADB supported FINCA Bank Georgia with the development of a digital field application tool to help the bank with remote onboarding of farmers in rural areas and to give small businesses and farmers access to credit. Since the introduction of the tool, the quality of the loan review process for the bank has continued to improve and the business started to realize the scale of its benefits, including use of an automized score card and system for centralized underwriting. This has greatly simplified access to finance for many FINCA Bank Georgia customers.

### Papua New Guinea: Digital Access Tool
Working with MiBank and Women's MicroBank, with support from the central bank, the Bank of Papua New Guinea (BPNG), ADB is piloting a biometric identification (ID) system for financial inclusion. This system works both online and offline to enable faster onboarding of clients in remote areas, where people often have no means of identifying themselves. Recognizing that the digital ID system can help drive financial inclusion across the economy, the BPNG is working on making amendments to the prudential standard in customer due diligence, which includes a framework for electronic know your customer (KYC), expanding existing requirements for customers deemed low-risk.

### The Philippines: Cloud Technology for Core Banking and Financial Inclusion
In collaboration with the central bank, the Banko Sentral ng Pilipinas, ADB has supported Cantilan Bank through a two-phased digital transformation pilot program. The focus of this program has been the migration of Cantilan Bank's core banking system to the cloud, and the integration of third-party systems, use of tablet hardware for increased field mobility and end-user services such as automated teller machine withdrawals, bill payments, and online and/or merchant payments. Cantilan Bank became the Philippines' first bank to operate its core systems in the cloud. This paved the way for 46 other financial institutions to gain central bank approval to develop their own cloud-based core banking systems. The central bank, as the main regulatory body, drove change by encouraging innovative technology solutions through the use of a regulatory sandbox and by providing guidance on the use of new technology, such as cloud technology. Under the second phase of this pilot program, ADB will support the development of an application program interface layer in a mobile banking channel that will provide users a secure and convenient means of accessing their accounts.

Source: L. Cipriano. 2021. Building Inclusive Digital Economies for Financial Inclusion. Presentation at the 2021 Asia–Pacific Financial Inclusion Forum. 25 May. https://drive.google.com/file/d/1rKGhL9vAUuAkduWlBY8Hc0_uRQPDiC06/view (accessed 15 November 2021).

By adopting technology solutions now, microfinance providers have a better chance of continuing to provide important services to clients during the COVID-19 crisis and support economic recovery, while also positioning themselves to operate more effectively after the pandemic. Table 1 summarizes examples of the areas microfinance providers can consider prioritizing for digital transformation to be successful.

### Table 1: Digital Transformation Priorities for Microfinance Providers

| | |
|---|---|
| Strengthening call center operations | In response to branch closures, upgrade infrastructure to address substantial increases in customers contacting, and being contacted by, microfinance providers. Additionally, ensure flexibility to operate contact centers with remote agents to be able to continue operating effectively in the event of work-from-home policies or government-enforced movement restrictions. |
| Digitizing customer interactions | Enable remote customer interactions through digital communication channels such as short messaging service (SMS) and over-the-top messaging (i.e., social media), to maintain robust customer relationships during periods where in-person interactions are restricted. |
| Delivering customer education on digital financial services | Complement digitization with corresponding digital education solutions for clients to ensure that they are capable of benefiting from digital (or digitally enhanced) products and services. |
| Digitizing core banking processes | Identify core banking processes that can be digitized for immediate and future value (i.e., electronic know your customer [eKYC], digital signature capture, online document upload solutions, etc.). |
| Addressing the agent network liquidity challenge | Ensure that customers have continued access to cash-in and cash-out services during branch closures through digitally delivered liquidity products for agents. |

Source: Adapted from J. Kirton. 2020. From Response to Recovery: How the COVID-19 Crisis Will Accelerate Digitization in Microfinance. *FINCA Ventures*. https://fincaventures.com/from-response-to-recovery-how-the-covid-19-crisis-will-accelerate-digitization-in-microfinance/ (accessed 3 March 2021).

Instead of relying on the poor to have access to technology directly, including the capabilities necessary to utilize it effectively, microfinance providers could build their own capabilities and act as intermediaries to help clients connect to the digital economy. For example, a microfinance institution might utilize technology to enable clients to access a cheaper and broader range of digital financial products and services through field officers, or to connect with e-commerce platforms and logistics networks to expand market opportunities. With this approach, they could also help clients mitigate new risks associated with the digital economy, many of which are greater for the poor, and include privacy breaches, fraud, transaction errors, or service interruptions.

## Financial Market Infrastructure Priorities to Accelerate Recovery and Resilience

There is no one-size-fits-all to how governments should prioritize their investments in financial market infrastructure development. However, there is greater convergence across governments and economies on principals to meaningfully reach those at the base of the economy. Each economy has its own unique challenges and advantages that have played a role in developments, so variance between economies across Asia and the Pacific is wide.

With regard to digital financial inclusion, key policy and infrastructure considerations can successfully raise digital financial inclusion safely and competitively. The United Nations Secretary-General's Special Advocate for Inclusive Finance for Development (UNSGSA 2019) has identified prerequisites for fintech, as a key accelerator for digital solutions, to be inclusive. These include data privacy, cybersecurity, digital identification, fair competition, physical infrastructure (I.e., agent networks), connectivity, interoperability, and financial and digital literacy. While each represents an important goal for governments, the COVID-19 pandemic has highlighted that certain structural features have proven critical for governments to implement rapid and effective responses to the crisis, including supporting vulnerable groups.

According to the COVID-19 Policy Database, ADB member economies have announced more than $30 trillion in funding to combat the pandemic, with nearly $4 trillion committed by developing economies (ADB 2021c).[7] The overall efficiency and effectiveness of these fiscal measures, and in particular their effectiveness in providing relief to those in the informal economy, has been put to the test throughout the crisis and exposed critical gaps in financial market infrastructure. White et al. (2021) examined these gaps and the opportunities they represent for improvement, and identified three financial infrastructure features of particular importance to the success of fiscal interventions: digital payment channels, basic digital identification (ID), and simple data on individuals and businesses linked to the ID.

White et al. (2021) concluded that economies with these three digital infrastructure features already were able to implement fiscal interventions with greater efficiency and effectiveness. Furthermore, the research found that emerging economies have higher economic value at stake from using digital financial infrastructure to support government disbursements. By enabling more direct, targeted, and efficient economic stimulus during the pandemic, development of these infrastructure features will not only enable greater support for economic recovery and meeting the immediate needs of the base of the economy, but will also help citizens to be more resilient to future shocks.

---

[7]   The ADB COVID-19 Policy Database is available online at: https://covid19policy.adb.org/.

## Digital Payments Channels

As the early stages of the COVID-19 pandemic unfolded with lockdowns and mobility restrictions, digital payments in many economies shifted from novelty to necessity. Besides enabling people to facilitate financial transactions remotely (sending money, making payments online, etc.), digital payments systems have proven crucial during the crisis to facilitate G2P social payments that provide immediate relief to individuals and businesses. While many governments have taken steps to accelerate the development of digital payments systems to meet these needs, people on low income, who generally rely more on cash to meet daily needs, have been disproportionately impacted.

To assist governments and other stakeholders with the complex task of developing inclusive digital payments systems, the Better Than Cash Alliance (2016) created a set of core principles to promote responsible practices in the move from cash to digital payments. These guide stakeholders on critical issues such as treating users fairly, ensuring funds are protected and accessible, prioritizing women, safeguarding client data, optimizing user experience, transparency, interoperability, and providing effective recourse mechanisms and value chain accountability. To implement this responsible agenda in digital payments, stakeholders need to ensure that even the non-tech layers are adequately recognized; governance and community in particular. These are critical in determining the benefits and potential negative impacts, as well as enabling continuous development of greater safeguards as feedback from all stakeholders is assessed.

In response to the rapid increase in demand for digital payments through the pandemic, the Better Than Cash Alliance has adapted the responsible practice principles to the immediate risks associated with delivering digital transfers. It has identified seven key lessons for responsible practices that stakeholders should prioritize to help ensure these systems can achieve inclusiveness and benefit the poorest and most vulnerable groups (Table 2).

*"Through the government's PromptPay initiative, a robust payments system had already been developed prior to the COVID-19 pandemic which has proven to be critical in enabling citizens to continue transacting safely and securely during the crisis."* Nawaron Dejsuvan, Assistant Governor, Financial Institutions Policy Group, Bank of Thailand

### Table 2: Lessons from COVID-19 for Improving Digital Payments

| Key Lesson | Description | Potential Solutions |
|---|---|---|
| 1. Create responsive complaint and feedback channels. | Digital financial transfer recipients need to have easy access to complaints and feedback mechanism systems so that their problems can be identified and addressed. | • Governments and cash transfer programs to set requirements and define responsibilities to address grievances in real time<br>• Regulation that sets and enforces minimum standards<br>• Service providers to ensure that feedback and complaints channels are applicable to users with low literacy or limited digital experience |
| 2. Deepen financial and digital literacy. | Recipients of government benefits are often low-income individuals or businesses with limited or no exposure to digital payments, which often make it difficult for many recipients to fully understand and access digital services. | • Governments can partner with the private sector or NGOs to establish education campaigns targeting specific capacity challenges. |

*(continued on next page)*

*(Table 2 continued)*

| Key Lesson | Description | Potential Solutions |
|---|---|---|
| 3. Spread information to increase inclusivity. | Numerous factors can contribute to the exclusion of individuals from digital transfer programs such as lack of ID, living in rural areas, limited information about eligibility criteria and enrollment information or limited agent network outreach. | • Regulators should ensure that social welfare programs are inclusive with information available to all.<br>• Governments need to digitize the building blocks for enrollment.<br>• Working with the private sector, governments can leverage existing technology (i.e., mobile phones) and networks (i.e., telecoms, utilities, etc.) to expand outreach and help people gain access to digital payments. |
| 4. Learn from transaction failures and proactively solve for them | Transaction failures can occur for a variety of reasons including poor connectivity, poor system performance, or mismatch in biometrics/identities due to poor-quality ID systems. | • Digital transfer programs should actively collect transaction failure rates as part of daily key performance indicators and track reasons for failure.<br>• Contingency plans, including the provision of non-digital alternatives if necessary, should also be developed. |
| 5. Disseminate information about cash-out points widely | Most digital transfer recipients, particularly at the base of the economy, will ultimately require cash. | • Governments and the private sector could collaborate on developing a platform that maps cash-in cash-out points across various service providers. |
| 6. Avoid overcharging and monitor during crisis | Operational and pricing rules for digital payments transactions can lead to overcharging (including the potential for agents to charge customers fees they are not subject to). | • Regulators could conduct spot checks to monitor instances of overcharging and require customer protection clauses be integrated into agents' contracts.<br>• Private sector participants should provide clear pricing guidelines and work with government agencies to establish appropriate transparency and remuneration plans for agents. |
| 7. Observe social distancing | Social distancing is expected to remain a necessity for cash-in and cash-out points to avoid ongoing health and safety risks. | • Governments should provide clear advice and protective equipment to agents.<br>• In collaboration with the private sector, governments can increase digital transaction limits to reduce the need for cash-out services.<br>• Governments can remove or reduce digital transaction fees to encourage people to keep funds digital. |

ID = identification, NGO = nongovernment organization.

Source: Adapted from Y. Xiao and K. N. Massally. 2021. *7 Lessons COVID-19 Taught Us About Improving Digital Payments.* Geneva: World Economic Forum. https://www.weforum.org/agenda/2021/01/davos-agenda-digital-payments-7-lessons-covid-19-taught-us/ (accessed 3 March 2021).

## Digital Identification

One of the most challenging obstacles in bridging the "payment divide" is lack of formal identity. As many as 1 billion people globally, mostly women and children, struggle to formally identify themselves, which severely prohibits access to formal financial products and services (ADB 2018). Establishment of digital identification systems, including economy-wide digital identification, is a crucial component of a safe and effective digital economy that is also inclusive. However, inclusion does not just mean that everyone (including the poor, informal and migrant workers, people living in remote areas, and refugees) can register, but also that everyone has the capability and opportunity to use their digital identification to receive assistance and empower themselves economically (Pangestu 2020). According to White et al. (2019), the economic value of developing a "good" digital identity system is significant (Box 2), and can bring up to a 90% reduction in customer onboarding costs or unlock value worth as much as 6% of GDP in developing economies.

---

**Box 2: Attributes of a "Good" Digital Identity System**

**To fully realize the potential of digital ID, well-governed controls are needed to mitigate the risks. Core elements of good digital ID include:**

**1** **Verified to a high degree of assurance:** meets both government and private sectors' standards for initial registration and subsequent acceptance for multiple important civic and economic uses

**2** **Unique:** an individual has only one identity within a scheme, and every scheme identity corresponds to only one individual

**3** **Established with individual consent:** individuals knowingly register for and use digital ID, with knowledge over what personal data will be captured and how they will be used

**4** **Protects user privacy and ensures control over personal data:** built-in safeguards ensure privacy and security while users have access to their personal data, know who else can access it, and have decision rights over that data

ID = identity.

Source: McKinsey Global Institute. 2019. Infographic: What is Good Digital ID? https://www.mckinsey.com/business-functions/mckinsey-digital/our-insights/infographic-what-is-good-digital-id (accessed 3 March 2021).

---

With many governments focusing on direct payments to low-income individuals or micro businesses for needed relief from the COVID-19 pandemic impacts, the importance of digital identification systems, including effective methods for verification and authentication, comes into sharper focus. For example, Chile's Cuenta Rut or Thailand's PromptPay services have made it possible for governments to mobilize social payments with rapid speed. A key component for success, including getting payments to low-income and informal workers, was their advantage of having access to domestic digital identity systems that could determine eligibility and allow deposits to go directly to accounts linked to their digital identity (Rutkowski et al. 2020). Not only can digital identification bring better efficiency and higher output for social transfers, it can also reduce risks including lowering rates of fraud by as much as 80% (White et al. 2021).

## Linking and Sharing Data

As more people gain access and engage with digital technology as part of their daily activities, the increasing generation of information is resulting in data-rich economies. How data are collected, stored, and used has a significant impact on the effectiveness of the digital economy, including how inclusive it is. Linking data, even very basic information, to digital identities is crucial to making digital identity systems function and creating additional value to users. For example, data on occupation, place of residence, mobile phone records or biometrics can be used to verify and authenticate individuals or businesses.

Referring to India's experience with developing digital financial infrastructure, D'Silva et al. (2019) pointed out that one of the guiding principles for India's approach to financial innovation was to ensure that "citizens should be empowered by the wealth that their data generates" (p. 106). Recognizing that data trails such as evidence of income or enterprise revenues and earning potential could help customers access broader financial services, the government has sought to give Indian citizens easy access and control over their data, including power to determine which institutions can see it. This is being achieved through its Aadhaar system, which has enabled 95% of the population to obtain a digital identity (Agarwal 2019), and spurred the development of digital platforms for basic services (payments, document storage, etc.). As explained by Nilekani (2018), these digital platforms are collectively known as the "India Stack" and regarded as a public good that enables governments and businesses to deliver paperless, cashless, and remote services. The India Stack, combined with Aadhaar, importantly enables people to access and exchange their data safely and leverage it to negotiate access to products and services such as credit, health care, education, or welfare benefits (Nilekani 2018). Other information showcasing the experiences of India and the Philippines in developing digital ecosystems that have enabled more effective government responses to the COVID-19 pandemic are provided in Case Studies 3 and 4.

### Case Study 3: The Role of India's Financial Inclusion Foundation in Providing COVID-19 Relief

The Government of India's ability to support its citizens through the ongoing pandemic is greatly boosted by being underpinned by financial inclusion programs that started years ago. Much of this began with the National Mission for Financial Inclusion, also known as the Prime Minister's Pradhan Mantri Jan Dhan Yojana initiative and launched in 2014. This program was instrumental in establishing the foundation upon which the government has been able to leverage for providing direct and rapid relief to citizens during the crisis. The initiative focuses on financial inclusion development across three pillars:

(i)    **Banking the unbanked.** Specifically, this involves reaching those at the base of the economy. To-date, the program has led to opening of about 428 million basic no-frills accounts for previously unbanked adults (known as Jan Dhan accounts).

(ii)   **Securing the unsecured.** This entails providing micro insurance benefits to those previously excluded.

(iii)  **Funding the unfunded.** This involves providing self-help groups and micro, small, and medium-sized enterprises with loans and credit guarantees.

In 2015, the government launched the Digital India program to accelerate digital transformation and further empower society.

The JAM trinity (Jan Dhan accounts, Aadhaar national identity program numbers, and mobile connections) has enabled a significant increase in financial access to the most rural parts of the economy where people can access not only their bank accounts but also make digital payments using the simple Aadhaar (or national identity number) that most of India's population now has.

In response to the COVID-19 pandemic, the government initiated two new major programs. The first was a relief and rehabilitation program that was launched in April 2020 at the beginning of the outbreak. Its intention was to provide immediate relief to those sections of society that had suffered most during lockdowns. It can be summarized by its four main components:

(i)    **Distributing direct cash to the accounts of women Jan Dhan account holders.** Under the program, about 200 million women account holders received small sums of money (totaling about $4 billion) to support daily needs while without access to their regular incomes.

(ii)   **Providing rapid cash access and transfer subsidies to the accounts of farmers.** This was critical to mitigate losses in agricultural produce during the harvest season. Under this program, the government was able to initiate rapid transfer subsidies and direct cash transfers to more than 90 million farmers across the economy.

(iii) **Ensuring frontline health workers had access to basic insurance facilities**. A large number of frontline workers were insured using direct digital platforms.

(iv) **Supporting small street vendors across the economy who had lost access to their livelihood and income due to lockdowns**. Through the Prime Minister's Street Vendor's AtmaNirbhar Nidhi program (PM SVANidhi) street vendors can access small ticket loans guaranteed by the government. All aspects of this scheme, including loan application and disbursement from the banks, is conducted through a digital platform.

This immediate relief and rehabilitation program has since been succeeded by the Prime Minister's Self Sufficiency program that aims to scale up access to affordable credit (guaranteed by the government) for micro, small, and medium-sized enterprises or other vulnerable segments, as well as initiatives to encourage agriculture and animal husbandry infrastructure development including loan schemes delivered through digital platforms.

Through these programs, the government of India has been able to respond to challenges and hardships faced by its citizens across different segments of society.

COVID-19 = coronavirus disease.
Source: S. Kaushik. 2021. Remarks at the 2021 Asia-Pacific Financial Inclusion Forum. 25 May.

## Case Study 4: Developing the Digital Financial Infrastructure in the Philippines

The COVID-19 pandemic has highlighted the strategic importance and practical value of digital financial inclusion. Recognizing that digitally enabled innovations in financial services offer great potential in achieving financial inclusion goals, the Bangko Sentral ng Pilipinas (BSP), the central bank of the Philippines, has taken action beyond creating an inclusive regulatory environment and has progressed plans to address impediments to digital financial inclusion, including to develop the financial infrastructure (i.e., digital connectivity, digital identity and payments ecosystem), accelerate financial education in targeted sectors, and promote consumer protection to improve consumer outcomes.

Examining the development of the digital financial infrastructure specifically, the BSP has provided strong support for programs that will hasten the establishment of reliable internet infrastructure across the economy. This includes passage of the Open Access in Data Transmission Act. This act liberalizes the ICT industry by, among others, lowering entry barriers and simplifying the licensing process for broadband network providers.

The BSP also led the issuance of amendments to the Executive Order No. 127, which liberalizes access to satellite technology and facilitates an instant, ready-to-deploy internet infrastructure for areas that are currently unserved and underserved by incumbent providers.

Support for digital payments is provided through the National Retail Payments System, a policy and regulatory framework for promoting safe, efficient, and reliable retail transactions. Under the NRPS, establishment of two Automated Clearing Houses (ACH) represent a major advancement in digital payments in the Philippines. The first, the Philippine EFT System and Operations Network (PESONet), was launched in 2017 to provide a more inclusive platform for electronic fund transfers and to allow small industry players to participate in the formal retail payments system. The second ACH, InstaPay, was launched in 2018 to facilitate small value payments, including for e-commerce, to better support the growth and development of micro, small, and medium-sized enterprises (BSP 2021).

With regard to digital identity, the BSP strongly supports the Philippine Identification System Act (PhilSys) by steering the creation of necessary policies, guidelines and standards; particularly about the effective implementation of electronic Know Your Customer (eKYC) in the finance sector to promote financial inclusion. As a digital identification system, the PhilSys is a key financial inclusion enabler as it addresses the oft-cited challenges of proper identification and catalyzes innovation in digital finance.

COVID-19 = coronavirus disease, ICT = information and communication technology.
Source: C. Fonacier. 2021. Remarks at the 2021 Asia-Pacific Financial Inclusion Forum. 25 May.

## Facilitating Innovative Approaches to Financial Inclusion

Rapid digitalization due to the COVID-19 pandemic has created new opportunities for digital financial services and new methods for regulatory compliance and supervision. However, making these available to the world's 1.7 billion unbanked population (Demirgüç-Kunt et al. 2018), and importantly, ensuring these services have a positive impact on the welfare and livelihoods of people living in poverty will require innovative approaches. Financial inclusion needs to go beyond formal access and incorporate critical enablers such as financial and digital literacy, technological infrastructure, trust in financial firms and regulators, and competitive choice (Zetzsche et al. 2020).

COVID-19 recovery strategies should address the role of governments in facilitating innovation in financial services. These strategies should incorporate plans to stimulate innovation by enhancing the development of an enabling policy and regulatory ecosystem for digital finance and fintech innovation, balanced with greater financial stability and consumer protection encouraging greater private and public sector cooperation.

### Developing an Ecosystem for Digital Transformation

Arner, Buckley, and Zetzsche (2018), in examining digital financial inclusion initiatives from a range of developing, emerging, and developed economies, found that successful support for digital transformation and achieving the full potential of fintech for financial inclusion require key underlying financial infrastructure components, supported by an enabling policy and regulatory environment. Their proposed framework, developed upon common characteristics of most successful digital financial inclusion initiatives, is built on a foundation of digital access; the importance of ensuring digital access to the widest possible proportion of the population. Four major pillars (summarized in Figure 4) outline the requirements for a digital financial ecosystem for economies to maximize the benefits of fintech-enabled financial inclusion.

Arner, Buckley, and Zetzsche (2018) concluded that it is the combination of the features represented in each pillar that enables successful digital financial inclusion. Each pillar is part of a broader ecosystem with interdependent elements. Having this is in place makes it possible to progress key digital services, including the digitization of government payments and services—crucial during the ongoing COVID-19 crisis. Furthermore, it reduces the cost of customer acquisition, making it easier for new fintech business models to enter the market.

### Developing an Enabling Policy and Regulatory Environment

Establishing an enabling policy and regulatory environment for financial inclusion has been a topic of much debate since the microfinance movement began in the 1970s. More recently, as digital technology and fintechs began disrupting traditional financial services, discussions on an enabling environment have shifted toward the need to accelerate innovation and create opportunities to utilize new technology

Figure 4: Framework for a Digital Financial Inclusion Ecosystem

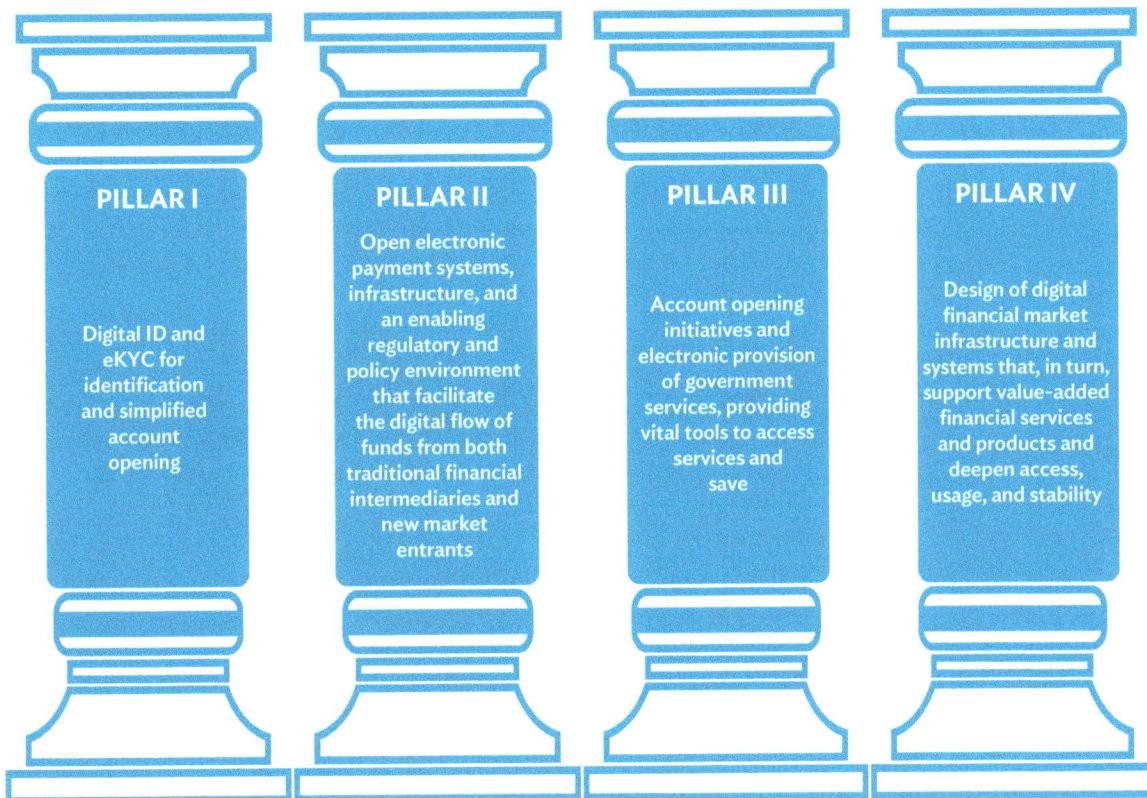

**PILLAR I**

Digital ID and eKYC for identification and simplified account opening

**PILLAR II**

Open electronic payment systems, infrastructure, and an enabling regulatory and policy environment that facilitate the digital flow of funds from both traditional financial intermediaries and new market entrants

**PILLAR III**

Account opening initiatives and electronic provision of government services, providing vital tools to access services and save

**PILLAR IV**

Design of digital financial market infrastructure and systems that, in turn, support value-added financial services and products and deepen access, usage, and stability

eKYC = electronic know your customer, ID = identification.

Source: Adapted from D. W. Arner, R. P. Buckley, and D. A. Zetzsche. 2018. Fintech for Financial Inclusion: A Framework for Digital Financial Transformation. *UNSW Law Research Paper. No. 18-87. University of Hong Kong Faculty of Law Research Paper* No. 2019/001, *University of Luxembourg Law Working Paper. No. 004-2019.* https://papers.ssrn.com/sol3/papers.cfm?abstract _id=3245287 (accessed 2 June 2021).

more effectively. Such innovation has not only led to significant breakthroughs in new delivery channels and products, it has drawn nonfinancial players into the finance sector (Beck 2020).

These disruptions to the finance sector challenge governments to establish and maintain an ecosystem that enables innovative approaches to financial inclusion while providing adequate protection for consumers, financial stability, and market integrity. Zetzsche et al. (2020, p. 5) proposed seven stages of a smart regulatory approach to developing ecosystems which enable safe fintech innovation (Figure 5). This focuses on sequenced reforms, informed by global best practice, which policy makers could prioritize to enable fintech innovation in ways that will accelerate financial inclusion, competition, and economic development:

(i) **Abolition of unsuitable regulation.** Regulators identify and modernize unsuitable regulation based on a regulatory impact assessment that determines whether legacy rules remain useful.

(ii)  **Proportional regulation.** Proportional regulation, reflected in provisions for market stability and integrity depending on the extent of risks underlying the regulated activity, create supportive pathways for new, particularly inclusive nonbank financial services.

(iii) **Innovation hub.** An Innovation Hub with experts of regulatory authority is best-suited to guide fintech firms through the regulatory maze, yield valuable insights into market innovations, and assess possibilities of dispensation.

(iv)  **Testing and piloting environment.** Testing and piloting regimes allow to apply leniency in a wait-and-see or test-and-learn approach to assist innovative firms. Authorities can further decide to tolerate innovations by licensed institutions and possibly by start-ups by extending on a case-by-case basis waivers or no-action-letter which declare certain activities as permissible or suspend certain rules.

(v)   **Regulatory sandbox.** A regulatory sandbox, which standardizes the scope of testing and piloting, allows regulators to create a tightly defined safe space for granting dispensation from specific regulatory requirements for innovative firms that qualify.

(vi)  **Restricted license/special charter scheme.** Restricted licenses allow feasible innovative firms to further develop their client base and financial and operational resources in a controlled manner.

(vii) **Full license.** A full license is essential for innovative firms as size requires and permits. Over these stages, as regulatory rigor and costs increase so tend to do fintech firms' maturity and ability to cope with risks and compliance, while making sure licensed entities get to benefit from equal treatment.

Zetzsche et al. (2020) further explained that this particular reform sequence is important for many reasons. By cutting red-tape and introducing proportional regulation, the regulatory requirements can be based on the justification of risks and remove obstacles to service providers being able to operate effectively while still ensuring safety. These operations, including opportunities for regulators to learn, can then be strengthened through an innovation hub; testing and piloting and sandbox regimes that ultimately lead to restricted or full license regimes as new products are developed. As each sequence of regulatory approaches progresses, an important outcome should be the lowering of entry barriers for firms, resulting in greater innovation and market competition.

## Figure 5: Smart Regulatory and Market Approaches to Financial Technology Innovation

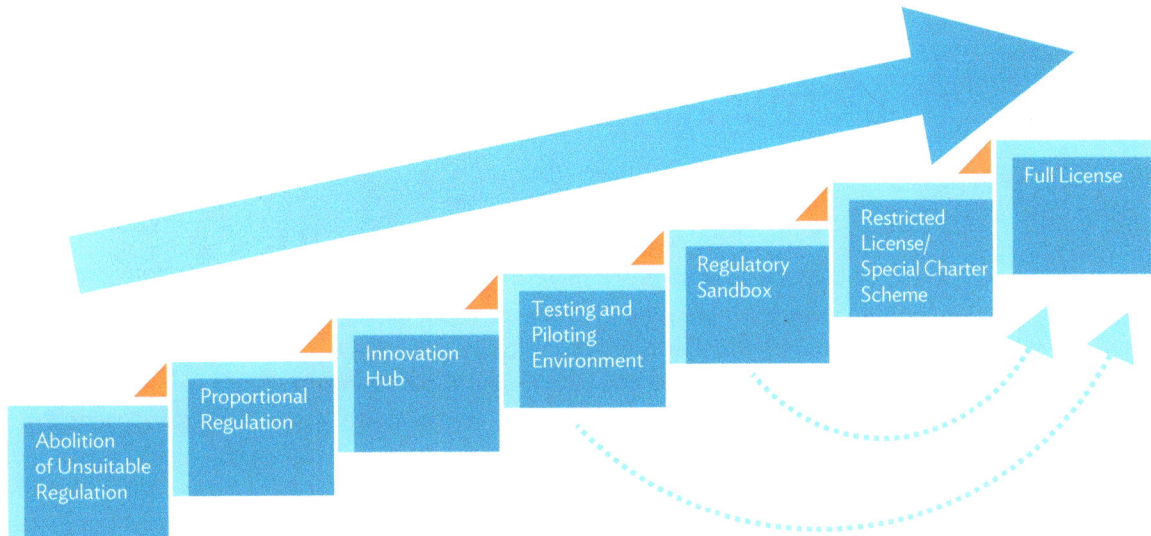

Abolition of Unsuitable Regulation

Proportional Regulation

Innovation Hub

Testing and Piloting Environment

Regulatory Sandbox

Restricted License/ Special Charter Scheme

Full License

Source: D. A. Zetzsche et al. 2020. *Fintech Toolkit: Smart Regulatory and Market Approaches to Financial Technology Innovation.* Bonn: Deutsche Gesellschaft für Internationale Zusammenarbeit (GIZ). https://papers.ssrn.com/sol3/papers.cfm?abstract _id=3598142 (accessed 7 March 2021).

# 4. EMERGING FINANCIAL INCLUSION CHALLENGES AND OPPORTUNITIES IN A WORLD DISRUPTED BY COVID-19

*"In the new economy being created by COVID-19, the adoption of digital technology is no longer a convenience, but has become a matter of necessity."* Chuchi Fonacier, Deputy Governor, Bangko Sentral ng Pilipinas

As technology developments continue to accelerate in response to the COVID-19 pandemic, governments will need to consider how these developments shape a post-COVID-19 world. The role of technology across multiple industries, including connecting people physically and virtually, will increase in importance and impact how people engage with financial products and services, and also health, education, energy, transport, and other services. As more services go digital, the demand for access to affordable, reliable, and safe digital infrastructure will also increase. From the supply side, use of big data and analytics will continue to be increasingly important for firms to remain competitive, and with significant amounts of new data becoming available, artificial intelligence and machine learning will feature prominently in how businesses achieve their goals. However, without proper planning and implementation, many of the expected benefits from technological advancements will continue to exclude poor and vulnerable groups in a post-COVID-19 world.

Regarding financial inclusion, one of the biggest stories to emerge from the pandemic will likely be how the fintech ecosystem has evolved throughout the crisis and the new opportunities and risks this has created. Fintechs are generally characterized as agile businesses that are capable of rapid delivery of new solutions. With the pandemic sparking a rise in demand for online or contactless payments, many fintechs will leverage their expertise in aspects such as onboarding, underwriting, and data visualization to work with other finance sector stakeholders and support the growing volumes of digital transactions (Deloitte 2020). As the expansion of digital services accelerates, policy makers and regulators need to consider how this will impact the financial inclusion landscape beyond the pandemic.

This section explores some of the potential new fintech impacts and opportunities that governments may need to consider, including the need to reassess the dimensions used to understand and monitor the impact of financial inclusion, regulatory concerns arising from a consolidated fintech marketplace and the growing importance of private sector collaboration, and new innovative fintech solutions that could help fund key infrastructure for digital financial inclusion.

## Reassessing How Financial Inclusion Is Understood

Financial inclusion is a multidimensional concept that is difficult to define and measure. Economies often apply unique definitions or perspectives for financial inclusion based on the characteristics of their finance sector or development priorities. As a result, the financial inclusion strategies of some economies may focus more on supporting enterprise development, while others emphasize improving the financial health of the poorest and most vulnerable in society. Despite varying perspectives, financial inclusion frameworks generally comprise key dimensions such as access and usage.

To account for the growing use of digital financial services in recent years, particularly during the COVID-19 pandemic, there is a growing interest to consider a new digital dimension to financial inclusion. For example, Khera et al. (2021) examined the impact of introducing a new digital dimension to a financial inclusion measurement index and found that the adoption of fintech has been key to driving financial inclusion. As digital finance is increasingly linked to progress in financial inclusion, it is becoming more important to understand its impact.

To examine this concept, Park and Mercado (2021) proposed a composite index for financial inclusion to better assess the varying significance of financial inclusion and its dimensions, assessing 153 advanced, emerging, and developing economies. They explored two innovations:

(i)   the inclusion of fintech infrastructure and financial development as key dimensions of financial inclusion; and

(ii)  considering the impact of various dimensions on socioeconomic outcomes across economic income groups.

The study's focus on dimensions, including new dimensions of fintech infrastructure and financial development (Table 4), is used to understand which elements of financial inclusion have the greatest impact on outcomes such as reducing poverty and income inequality, increasing women's empowerment, or supporting entrepreneurship. Furthermore, by also considering different economic income groups, a greater understanding of the extent of which these dimensions matter can be achieved. For example, developed economies may benefit from greater financial access or more efficient financial services enabling enterprises to attain optimal output—resulting in lower poverty and higher entrepreneurship.

*"New financial inclusion success indicators can be used to account for the evolving financial landscape including the increasing use of technology and its role in expanding the reach and quality of services to the poor."* Cyn-Young Park, Director, Regional Cooperation and Integration Division, Asian Development Bank

### Table 3: Dimensions of Financial Inclusion

| | |
|---|---|
| Access | Includes number of ATMs and bank branches per 100,000 adults, proportion of adult population with bank account, credit card, debit card, and mobile money account. |
| Financial Development | Includes ease of getting credit, bank concentration, financial system deposits to GDP, and depth of credit information. |
| Usage | includes proportion of adult population who borrowed and saved in a financial institution, and depositors in commercial banks per 1,000 adults. |
| Fintech Infrastructure | Includes share of adult population who made electronic and digital payments, number of fixed broadband and mobile cellular subscriptions per 100 persons, number of secure internet servers per 1 million people, share of adult population who used the internet to pay bills or buy something online, and internet bandwidth per internet user. |

ATM = automated teller machine, GDP = gross domestic product.

Source: Adapted from C. Park and R. Mercado, Jr. 2021. Understanding Financial Inclusion: What Matters and How it Matters. *ADBI Working Paper Series.* No. 1287. Tokyo: Asian Development Bank Institute. https://www.adb.org/publications/understanding-financial-inclusion-what-matters-and-how-it-matters.

Using computed financial inclusion and dimension indicators as regressors for socioeconomic outcomes, combined with similar estimations based on economic income groups, Park and Mercado (2021) have produced the following key findings:

- The impact of financial inclusion and its dimensions is largest for poverty.

- Not all dimensions are significant for specific socioeconomic outcomes (Figure 6).

- There is varying significance and impact across economic income groups (Figure 7).

### Figure 6: Financial Inclusion and Socioeconomic Outcomes

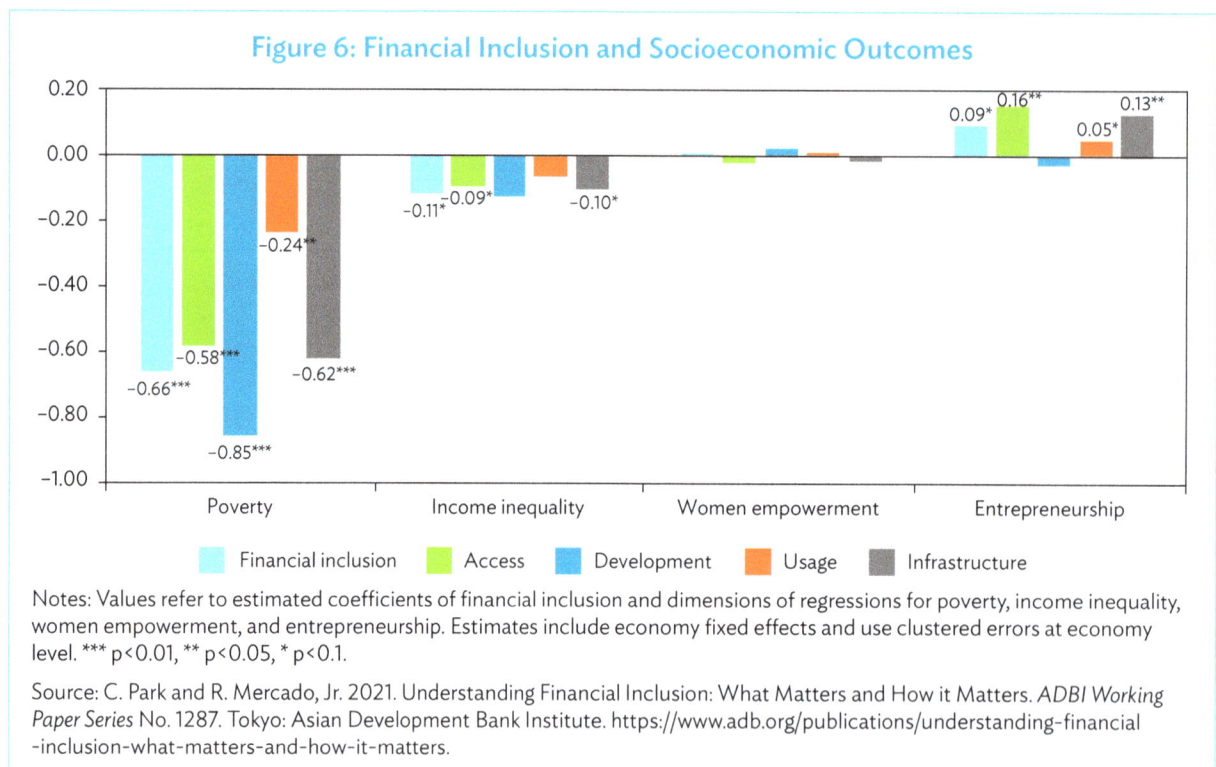

Notes: Values refer to estimated coefficients of financial inclusion and dimensions of regressions for poverty, income inequality, women empowerment, and entrepreneurship. Estimates include economy fixed effects and use clustered errors at economy level. *** p<0.01, ** p<0.05, * p<0.1.

Source: C. Park and R. Mercado, Jr. 2021. Understanding Financial Inclusion: What Matters and How it Matters. *ADBI Working Paper Series* No. 1287. Tokyo: Asian Development Bank Institute. https://www.adb.org/publications/understanding-financial -inclusion-what-matters-and-how-it-matters.

Figure 6 shows that financial inclusion and its dimensions are significantly associated with lower poverty. Furthermore, higher financial inclusion, access and fintech infrastructure have a significant impact on lowering income inequality, whereas greater financial inclusion, access, usage and fintech infrastructure significantly increase entrepreneurship.

When these dimensions are assessed by income groups, Figure 7 shows that financial inclusion has the most significant impact on lowering poverty in middle-income economies. Interestingly, while financial inclusion lowers income inequality for middle-income economies, it actually increases income inequality in high-income economies. The results provide further evidence that financial inclusion has a positive impact on women's empowerment and entrepreneurship in low-income economies.

### Figure 7: Financial Inclusion Outcomes, by Income Groups

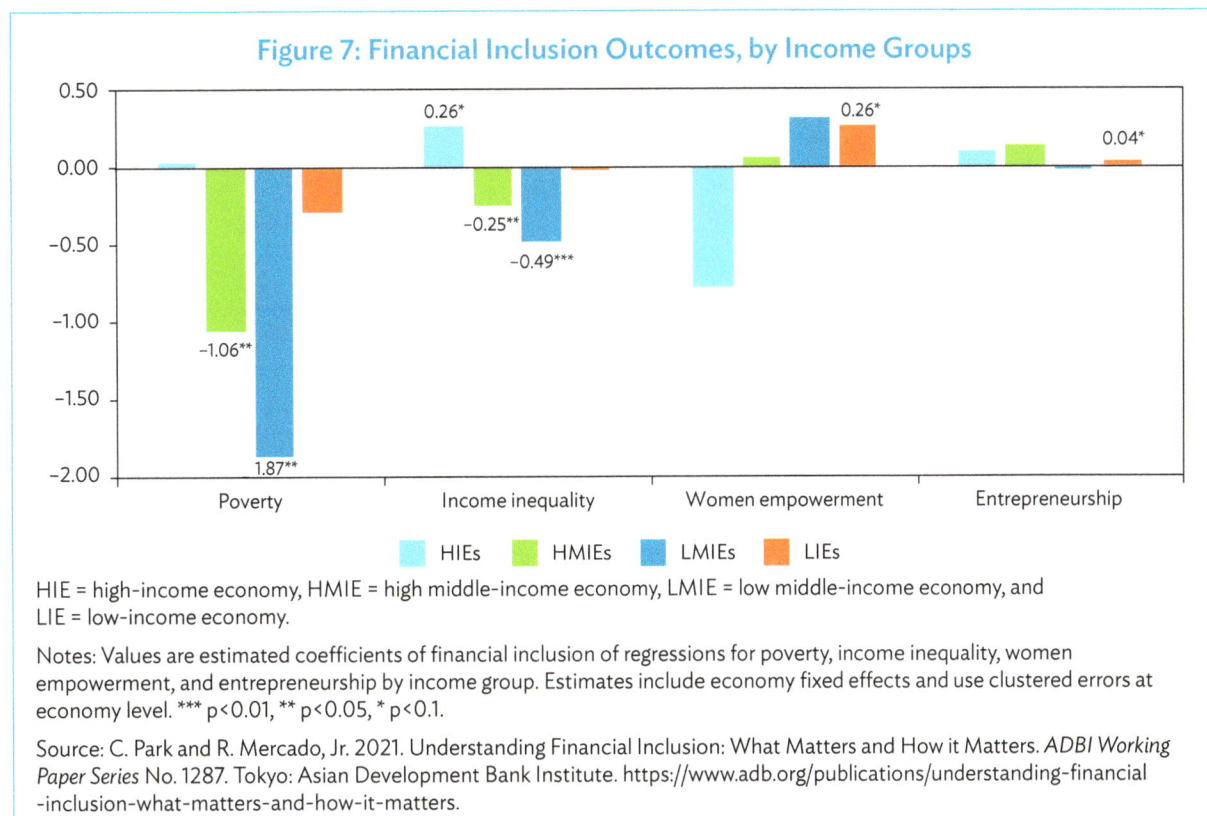

HIE = high-income economy, HMIE = high middle-income economy, LMIE = low middle-income economy, and LIE = low-income economy.

Notes: Values are estimated coefficients of financial inclusion of regressions for poverty, income inequality, women empowerment, and entrepreneurship by income group. Estimates include economy fixed effects and use clustered errors at economy level. *** $p<0.01$, ** $p<0.05$, * $p<0.1$.

Source: C. Park and R. Mercado, Jr. 2021. Understanding Financial Inclusion: What Matters and How it Matters. *ADBI Working Paper Series* No. 1287. Tokyo: Asian Development Bank Institute. https://www.adb.org/publications/understanding-financial-inclusion-what-matters-and-how-it-matters.

This new evidence highlights the importance of considering levels of economic development to understand the varying significance and impact of financial inclusion and its dimensions on socioeconomic outcomes. It further underscores the importance of continuing to assess the financial inclusion dimensions used in strategic frameworks to ensure that they remain relevant and capable of producing optimal results in a rapidly evolving environment. As an example, the Government of Indonesia has taken steps to improve outcomes by integrating its financial inclusion programs with strategies to boost economic activity (Case Study 5).

### Case Study 5: Integrating Economic Activity with Financial Inclusion in Indonesia

Indonesia faces challenging geographic and demographic conditions for financial inclusion that are exacerbated by limited infrastructure, low digital literacy, and urban and rural disparities. The Government of Indonesia views digital transformation as an opportunity to facilitate and accelerate the integration of economic and financial inclusion. To achieve this, the government has issued a new regulation on an economy-wide strategy for financial inclusion. This strategy focuses on six key outcomes:

(i)   increasing access to formal financial services;

(ii)   increasing literacy and protecting consumers;

(iii)   expanding the reach of financial services;

(iv)   strengthening access to capital and development support for micro, small, and medium-sized enterprises;

(v)   expanding digital financial products and services; and

(vi)   strengthening the integration of economic activities and inclusive finance through digital financial services.

*(continued on next page)*

*(Case Study 5 continued)*

To support progress toward the goals laid out in this strategy, Indonesia's central bank, Bank Indonesia, has developed a new policy approach focused on integrating economic activities and financial inclusion. The implementation of this policy is carried out under three pillars:

(i)    economic empowerment,

(ii)   broadening access to finance and literacy, and

(iii)  policy harmonization and synergy.

Bank Indonesia adopted this particular approach considering that most of Indonesia's population is at the base of the economy. As such, they have limited financial literacy and economic capacity. To ensure financial inclusion results in positive outcomes for people, Bank Indonesia's approach puts strong emphasis on supporting increased enterprise development and mentoring. This has proven even more important in recent years as a result of increased digital transformation throughout the economy and the opportunity for entrepreneurs to adopt technology solutions to enhance business outcomes.

Another key endeavor by Bank Indonesia is its support for open banking. Open banking APIs between banks, fintechs and other stakeholders can greatly speed up digitalization. Bank Indonesia has backed this by introducing the *Indonesia Payment System Blueprint 2025*. One of the visions it outlines is to ensure a strong link between fintechs and banks to contain the escalation of shadow-banking risks. Bank Indonesia has moved this forward by introducing regulation on the use of digital technology, including APIs, as well as on the partnership models between fintechs and banks. Through the framework set out in the blueprint, Indonesia hopes its payment systems will support broader integration of economic activity and financial inclusion while also fostering greater digital transformation in the banking industry. Furthermore, it hopes to help strike a balance between innovation, consumer protection, and market integrity and stability.

API = application program interface.
Source: Y. Resmi Sari. 2021. Remarks at the 2021 Asia-Pacific Financial Inclusion Forum. 25 May.

## The Evolving Fintech Landscape

While it is too early to assess how policy measures put in place to respond to the pandemic have impacted the fintech ecosystem, early insights show that payment companies appear to have benefited from rapid adoption through lockdowns and other measures to restrict movement (Le Moral 2020). Within the first quarter of 2021, Mastercard experienced a 1-billion increase in digital (i.e., contactless) transactions globally relative to the same period in 2020, including twofold growth in India and fourfold growth in Thailand (Strangio 2021). In the Philippines, digital payments surged by over 5,000% in 2020 amid the pandemic (Lucas 2021) including the volume of PESONet and InstaPay transactions increasing by 122% and increasing in value by 59% during the first quarter of the year (BSP 2020). Globally, the COVID-19 crisis is expected to accelerate the adoption of digital payments by as much as 10%, with the total estimated penetration of digital payments reaching 67% (MacArthur et al. 2020).

On the other hand, digital banks and digital lending have faced increased pressure as a result of the crisis. Consumption declines, rising unemployment, and repayment moratoriums have put undercapitalized lending companies at risk while digital banks have experienced significant drops in usage leading many to restructure their operations in an attempt stay afloat (Le Moral 2020). A decline in funding has also put increased pressure on companies yet to achieve scale, with investors cautious on the prospects of a recession (Sahay et al. 2020 and CB Insights 2020).

Despite these pressures, their low-cost and agile business models should allow fintechs to weather the storm. However, increased consolidation is expected, likely because smaller fintechs or those with thinner buffers would be unable to cope with the tightening of funding conditions, weakened demand, or a decline in transactions after the pandemic (Sahay et al. 2020), or if large banks recognize their own digital shortcomings during the crisis, and so accelerate the rate that incumbents buy up promising fintech firms as economies emerge from the pandemic (Ruddenklau 2020).

Another important factor that can reshape fintech dramatically is the extent to which BigTech enters the market for financial services.[8] Armed with vast data capabilities and customer knowledge, the possible rise of BigTech in finance is expected to take market share from less competitive incumbents. While BigTech has already begun offering financial services (particularly in the People's Republic of China), how far this can go will depend largely on the regulatory environment (OECD 2020a).

All these issues contribute to what could become widespread consolidation in the fintech industry and lead to greater market concentration. Regulators need to consider how concentration, including the potential emergence of a few dominant players, might reduce competition and importantly, how this might impact financial inclusion at the base of the economy.

## Partnerships to Address Evolving Needs

In response to the crisis, partnerships between technology providers and financial institutions have accelerated access to capital and other products and services to underserved populations. These private sector partnerships are also crucial for developing interoperable systems on a scale to achieve ubiquity and mass access to digital products and services. With the needs of customers evolving rapidly through the COVID-19 pandemic, especially given the rise in demand for digital or remote services offerings, the importance of such partnerships has grown exponentially.

However, as already noted, financial institutions have struggled to provide digital services to customers in poor and vulnerable segments of the population. Figure 8 explores this further by separating customer segments in Asia into three groups within a pyramid. The top of the pyramid (or "Penthouse") includes the top-tier financial institutions and "neo banks" (i.e., digital or online banks) leading in digitization and serving wealthy individuals or enterprises with sophisticated digital products. Most have developed high-cost technology which means there is little profit in moving down the pyramid to serve lower-income segments. Furthermore, most fintechs aim to engage with these top-tier institutions as an opportunity for quick and higher returns.

---

[8]    The term BigTech typically refers to large platform-based technology firms (such as Alibaba, Amazon, Apple, Google, or Rakuten).

Moving down the pyramid (i.e., the "Ground Floor"), a larger group of low-margin customers and MSMEs are served by smaller (nonbank) financial institutions—largely branch-based with no digital services. These financial institutions face several obstacles to going digital. They must also deal with increased competition from both larger banks attempting to come down the pyramid as well as digital disrupters such as Grab, Ant Financial, or FANG, which are offering digital financial or payments services. Currently, very few fintechs are focused on this segment of the market.

The base of the pyramid (i.e., the "Basement"), represents the estimated more than 1 billion people in the region who remain financially excluded (Bhardwaj et al. 2018). While this segment represents the largest growth opportunity, it is also the most challenging, given a wide range of issues such as low literacy rates, limited infrastructure, and lack of trust in technology. Key to meeting the needs of this market will be the development of low-cost and sustainable services that are basic (payments, micro-lending, and so on) and can bridge the gap between cash and digital transactions.

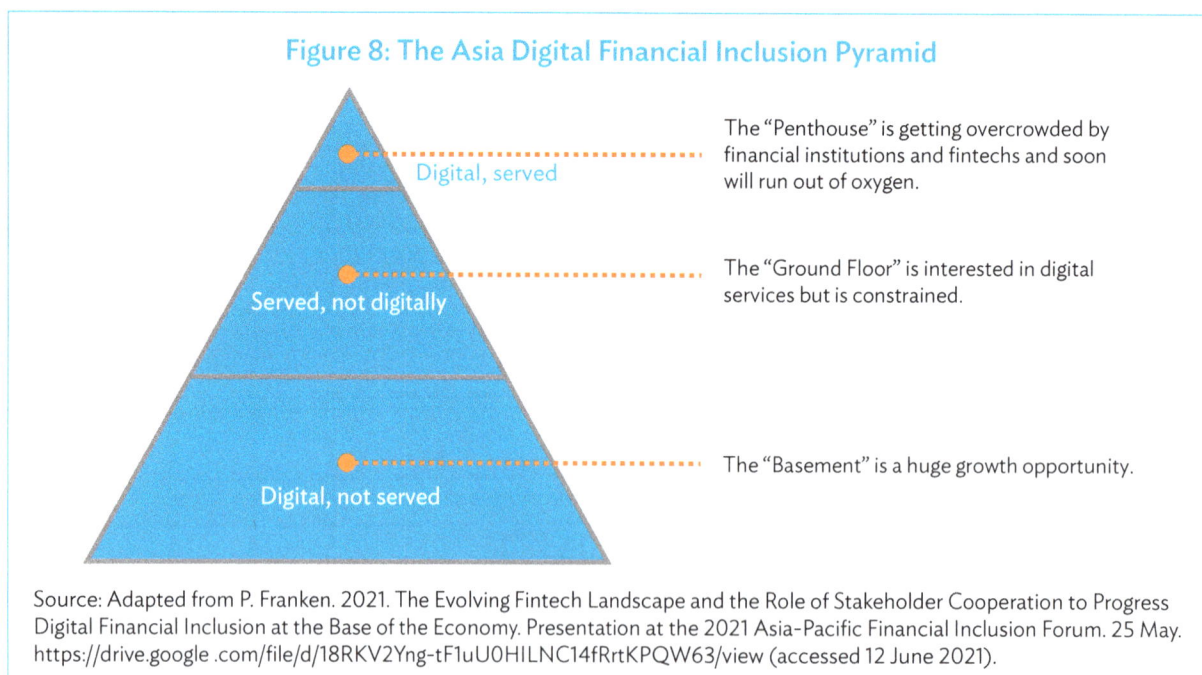

### Figure 8: The Asia Digital Financial Inclusion Pyramid

Digital, served — The "Penthouse" is getting overcrowded by financial institutions and fintechs and soon will run out of oxygen.

Served, not digitally — The "Ground Floor" is interested in digital services but is constrained.

Digital, not served — The "Basement" is a huge growth opportunity.

Source: Adapted from P. Franken. 2021. The Evolving Fintech Landscape and the Role of Stakeholder Cooperation to Progress Digital Financial Inclusion at the Base of the Economy. Presentation at the 2021 Asia-Pacific Financial Inclusion Forum. 25 May. https://drive.google .com/file/d/18RKV2Yng-tF1uU0HILNC14fRrtKPQW63/view (accessed 12 June 2021).

*"While there is a lot of new technology available in the market, many financial institutions are not yet ready for it. New partnerships will be crucial to accelerating technology adoption and achieving its full potential to address exclusion."* Pieter Franken, Director, The ASEAN Financial Innovation Network (AFIN)

Rather than operate in silos, which limits reach and opportunity, businesses can leverage their collective assets across the financial and technology ecosystem to make progress toward developing an inclusive digital economy and accelerating economic recovery (Magats 2020). While partnerships between key private sector stakeholders, including banks, fintechs, and mobile network operators, are becoming more common, more work is needed to ensure they result in greater financial inclusion, including enhanced opportunity and resilience among the poorest and most vulnerable.

In the case of microfinance providers, private sector partnerships can create opportunities for leveraging digital infrastructure to improve operations or customer services. On the other hand, larger entities such as banks, technology companies, or e-commerce platforms can benefit from partnerships with microfinance providers because they gain access to a unique and largely unserved customer base. However, microfinance providers may struggle because issues such as limited knowledge of technology advances or other trends impacting the broader ecosystem make it difficult for them to negotiate successfully with potential partners (Bull 2018). The API Exchange Platform represents a way to break the pattern (Case Study 6).

## Case Study 6: The APIX Platform—Facilitating Partnerships between Fintechs and Financial Institutions

Most fintechs in Asia will take up to 2 years before they can sell an offering to a bank. Recognizing financial institutions have been slow to adopt technology, in 2018 the IFC, World Bank, Monetary Authority of Singapore, and ASEAN Bankers Association created the APIX Platform to speed up adoption.

The purpose of the APIX Platform is to provide fintechs, financial institutions, and commercial actors with a space in the digital economy to explore opportunities for collaboration. To achieve this, the platform is designed to make it easier for financial institutions to adopt technology solutions by enabling them to explore the APIs and the potential use cases for technology being made available through participating fintechs. Importantly, the platform removes several barriers to enable financial institutions to digitize rapidly and for firms in the real sector to integrate financial solutions into their operations. Some examples of the solutions and support financial institutions can access through the platform include prefabricated "digital journeys" (i.e., digital systems which are already designed to support customer accessibility and usage), interoperability through fintech APIs published on the platform, partnerships with key technology companies (Amazon, Google, etc.) to support the transition to cloud services and links with other local financial institutions to leverage their ability to provide cash-in and cash-out services.

The combination of such multiple challenges often make it impossible for smaller financial institutions to achieve digitalization and take a more active role in digital transformation of the real economy and consumers' lives. To make the journey less daunting, the APIX Platform provides a planning framework known as the "APIX assisted 5-D and Two Phase approach," which aims to help financial institutions in developing a step-by-step strategy to digitalize rapidly. Key to the approach is how it encourages financial institutions to test solutions and determine best matches for their needs and the needs of customers.

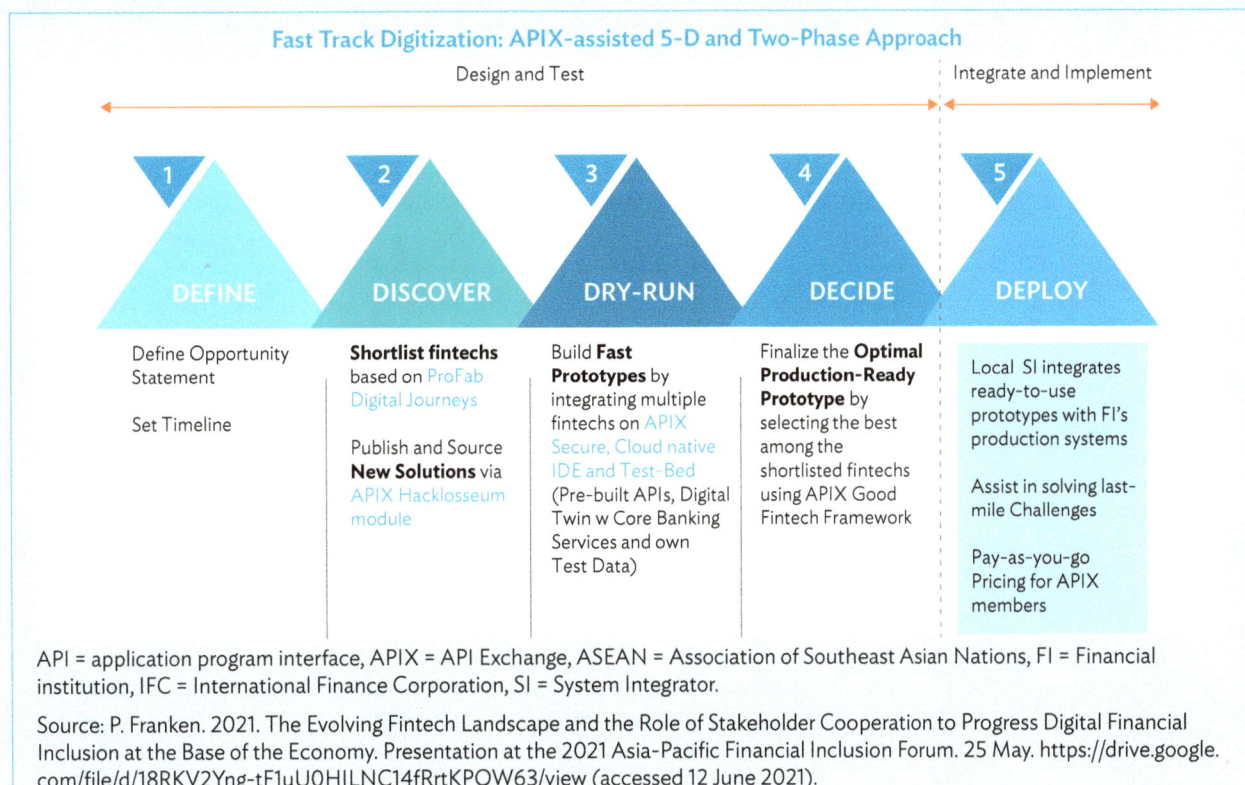

**Fast Track Digitization: APIX-assisted 5-D and Two-Phase Approach**

Design and Test | Integrate and Implement

| 1 DEFINE | 2 DISCOVER | 3 DRY-RUN | 4 DECIDE | 5 DEPLOY |
|---|---|---|---|---|
| Define Opportunity Statement<br><br>Set Timeline | **Shortlist fintechs** based on ProFab Digital Journeys<br><br>Publish and Source **New Solutions** via APIX Hacklosseum module | Build **Fast Prototypes** by integrating multiple fintechs on APIX Secure, Cloud native IDE and Test-Bed (Pre-built APIs, Digital Twin w Core Banking Services and own Test Data) | Finalize the **Optimal Production-Ready Prototype** by selecting the best among the shortlisted fintechs using APIX Good Fintech Framework | Local SI integrates ready-to-use prototypes with FI's production systems<br><br>Assist in solving last-mile Challenges<br><br>Pay-as-you-go Pricing for APIX members |

API = application program interface, APIX = API Exchange, ASEAN = Association of Southeast Asian Nations, FI = Financial institution, IFC = International Finance Corporation, SI = System Integrator.

Source: P. Franken. 2021. The Evolving Fintech Landscape and the Role of Stakeholder Cooperation to Progress Digital Financial Inclusion at the Base of the Economy. Presentation at the 2021 Asia-Pacific Financial Inclusion Forum. 25 May. https://drive.google.com/file/d/18RKV2Yng-tF1uU0HILNC14fRrtKPQW63/view (accessed 12 June 2021).

*"There is risk that persistent digital inequality will hinder financial inclusion efforts and deepen income and economic inequality."*
Ulrich Volz, Director of the Centre for Sustainable Finance, SOAS, University of London & Senior Research Fellow, German Development Institute

While partnerships within the private sector are important for meeting the needs of customers amid evolving conditions due to the COVID-19 pandemic, public–private partnerships are also critical for addressing emerging financial inclusion priorities, particularly providing urgent relief to citizens (i.e., facilitating social transfers) or speeding up recovery, such as by supporting micro, small, and medium-sized enterprise digitalization. Overall, private sector cooperation is expected to improve significantly because of the crisis as governments seek sustainable and resilient infrastructure solutions for their economic stimulus strategies (Fakhoury 2020).

## Emergence of Innovative Financing Mechanisms for Digital Infrastructure

Digital connectivity across Asia and the Pacific—supported by lower costs, better connection quality, increased adoption of online services, and the proliferation of smartphones—has experienced steady growth since the turn of the century with an estimated 1.7 billion people gaining access to the digital space between 2002 and 2018 (ADB 2021a). However, persistent subregional gaps remain, particularly in emerging economies where many at the base of the economy are still excluded. Closing the digital divide requires a multipronged approach, including lowering cultural and skills barriers, expanding access to technology, and improving digital infrastructure and connectivity.

Policy makers and regulators need to consider new risks associated with the digital divide that are emerging as the fintech industry responds to the COVID-19 pandemic. However, developments in the industry are also creating new opportunities for the delivery of high-quality digital financial services. One such opportunity is the potential for emerging fintech financing models to support key digital infrastructure developments necessary for digital financial inclusion at the base of the economy.

Digital infrastructure refers to an ecosystem of connected technology where the exchange of information is possible and digital systems are able to function effectively. This ecosystem is made up of hard and soft infrastructure that are strongly interdependent (Figure 9). Hard infrastructure includes transport and connectivity elements (i.e., optical fiber networks, communications satellites, mobile network towers, and the like) and processing and storage needs (such as data centers, cloud computing providers, content delivery providers). Soft infrastructure is defined as the required services and applications necessary to operate systems and networks (i.e., fintech, digital identity, or other e-platforms) and terminals and devices such as the smart grids, smart meters, or terminal devices such as mobile phones or computers used to optimize efficiency and sustainability (AIIB 2020a).

The lack of financial market development in the region continues to hinder mobilization of the region's savings on a scale to match its vast investment needs. Asia's investors continue to hold considerably more nonregional assets and liabilities than regional ones, with two-thirds of the region's assets and liabilities placed in nonregional economies as of the end of 2019 (ADB 2021). This is largely because

## Figure 9: Definition of Hard and Soft Infrastructure

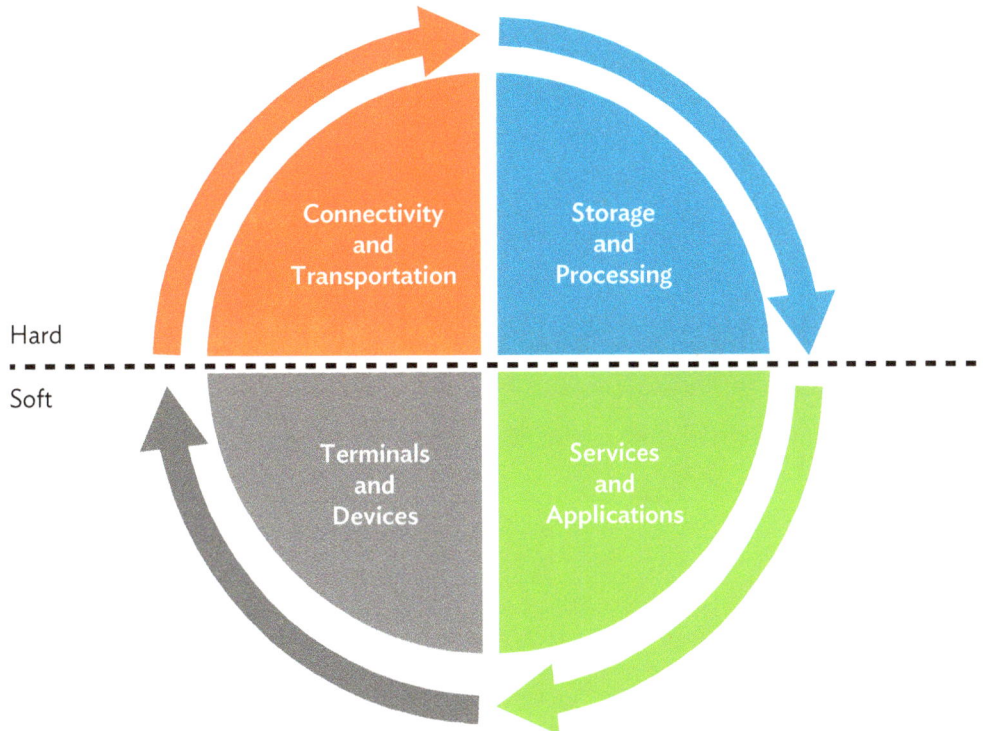

Source: Asian Infrastructure Investment Bank (AIIB). 2020. *Digital Infrastructure Sector Strategy: AIIB's Role in the Growth of the Digital Economy of the 21st Century*. Beijing. https://www.aiib.org/en/policies-strategies/operational-policies/digital-infrastructure-strategy/.content/_download/AIIB-Digital-Strategy.pdf (accessed 15 March 2021).

in the region deep and liquid financial markets are lacking, financial products and services are insufficient, and the institutional investor base is narrow. As a result, significant capital flows from Asia to advanced economies, often into low-yielding safe assets, limiting the potential to support economic growth locally including investments in the region's growing digital economy.

The digital economy is becoming one of the most important drivers of economic growth, especially for emerging markets, according to the Asian Infrastructure Investment Bank (2020b). Across the region's emerging and developing economies, expanding connectivity remains a priority (representing as much as 54% of the investment gap) with greater capital investments needed to improve mobile coverage, upgrade mobile networks, and expand fixed broadband, followed by investment to establish local data center infrastructure that supports locally deployed digital services. However, while the digital economy continues to grow significantly in size and economic significance, the annual financing gap for digital infrastructure, regarded as the backbone of the digital economy, is projected to widen significantly. The gap is prominent in Asia and is expected to reach as much as $512 billion by 2040, representing more than half the total investment gap worldwide (Figure 10). The overall annual infrastructure gap is estimated at $1.7 trillion for developing Asia (ADB 2017).

### Figure 10: Projected Growth of Digital Infrastructure Financing Gap
#### ($ billion)

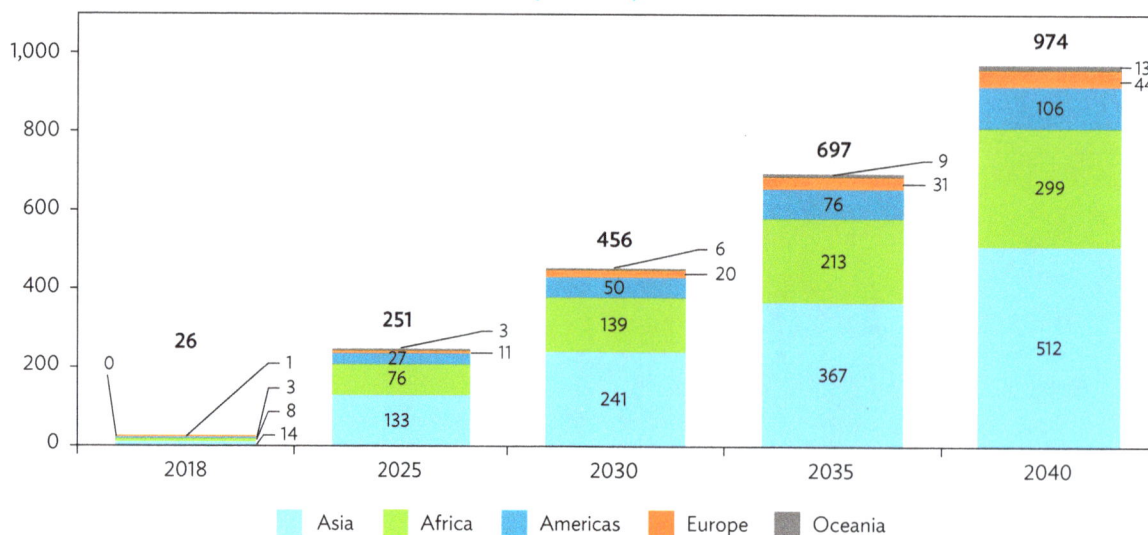

Source: World Economic Forum. 2018. *Financing a Forward-Looking Internet for All*. Geneva. http://www3.weforum.org/docs/WP_Financing_Forward-Looking_Internet_for_All_report_2018.pdf (accessed 24 July 2021).

Developing the region's capital markets to mobilize domestic savings and close the growing digital infrastructure investment gap will be critical to the success of digital financial inclusion. With net savings across Asia exceeding $400 billion (1.4% of GDP) in 2019 (Table 4), emerging fintech solutions present a promising opportunity to leverage technological advances to direct excess savings to where they are needed most. Accelerated by the COVID-19 pandemic, the pace of technological change is fueling innovative approaches and financing models with potential to solve these challenges (ADB 2021d). In this way, fintech can complement conventional capital markets' role in funding infrastructure necessary for digital financial inclusion.

Some examples of emerging fintech and blockchain solutions that could be leveraged for investment in the digital economy and digital financial systems include asset tokenization, blockchain-based project bonds, and crowdfunding. These examples—explained in further detail here—can have a positive impact by broadening the investor base, reducing transaction costs through disintermediation and automation, improving transparency, and reducing the size of liquidity requirements. This is achieved primarily through their ability to create a user-friendly investment process with easy access, enabling even small amounts from retail investors, as well as aggregating small-sized projects to attract institutional investors.

## Table 4: Savings and Investment—Asia, 2019

| Economies | Levels ($ billion) | | | % of GDP | | |
|---|---|---|---|---|---|---|
| | Savings | GDCF | Net Savings | Savings | GDCF | Net Savings |
| Asia | 10,819 | 10,396 | 423 | 36.3 | 34.9 | 1.4 |
| Japan | 1,514 | 1,326 | 188 | 29.4 | 25.8 | 3.7 |
| Emerging Asia | 8,703 | 8,459 | 244 | 39.2 | 38.1 | 1.1 |
| PRC | 6,257 | 6,176 | 81 | 43.8 | 43.3 | 0.6 |
| India | 836 | 851 | -15 | 29.1 | 29.7 | -0.5 |
| NIEs | 824 | 678 | 146 | 34.5 | 28.4 | 6.1 |
| Hong Kong, China | 91 | 69 | 22 | 25.0 | 18.9 | 6.1 |
| Korea, Republic of | 573 | 516 | 57 | 34.8 | 31.3 | 3.4 |
| Singapore | 159 | 92 | 67 | 42.8 | 24.9 | 18.0 |
| ASEAN-5 | 787 | 754 | 33 | 29.5 | 28.3 | 1.2 |
| Indonesia | 347 | 378 | -31 | 31.0 | 33.8 | -2.8 |
| Malaysia | 89 | 77 | 12 | 24.4 | 21.0 | 3.4 |
| The Philippines | 119 | 99 | 20 | 31.6 | 26.2 | 5.4 |
| Thailand | 171 | 130 | 41 | 31.5 | 24.0 | 7.5 |
| Viet Nam | 61 | 70 | -10 | 23.1 | 26.8 | -3.7 |

ASEAN = Association of Southeast Asian Nations, GDCF = gross domestic capital formation, GDP = gross domestic product, NIEs = newly industrialized economies, PRC = People's Republic of China.

Notes: (i) Asia (or Asia and the Pacific) refers to ADB's regional members (developing and advanced) with available data. Emerging Asia includes the PRC, India, NIEs, and ASEAN-5. (ii) Gross savings (current $) is calculated as gross national income less total consumption, plus net transfers. (iii) Gross domestic capital formation (current $) consists of outlays on additions to the fixed assets of the economy plus net changes in the level of inventories. Fixed assets include land improvements (fences, ditches, drains, and so on); plant, machinery, and equipment purchases; and the construction of roads, railways, and the like, including schools, offices, hospitals, private residential dwellings, and commercial and industrial buildings. Inventories are stocks of goods held by firms to meet temporary or unexpected fluctuations in production or sales, and "work in progress." According to the 1993 System of National Accounts, net acquisitions of valuables are also considered capital formation. (iv) Net savings: Gross savings minus gross domestic capital formation. (v) Japan figures and figures for net savings are for 2018.

Source: World Bank. 2021. World Development Indicators. https://databank.worldbank.org/home.aspx (accessed 26 July 2021).

## Asset Tokenization

Tokenizing assets is the process of issuing a blockchain security token which digitally represents a real tradable asset (Laurent et al. 2018). This allows the economic value and ownership rights of an asset to be converted into digital tokens and recorded on a distributed ledger (OECD 2020b). Tokens essentially represent portions of the asset (i.e., portions of the value of a painting, real estate, a company share, or other assets) that can then be sold as a "nonfungible" asset or traded on secondary markets.[9]

A key benefit of asset tokenization is its potential to increase efficiencies and fairness by greatly reducing the friction involved in the creation, buying, and selling of securities (Laurent et al. 2018). As per Tian et al. (2021), tokenization could

[9] A more detailed overview of asset tokenization and its potential in emerging markets can be found in Y. Tian et al. 2021. Asset Tokenization: A Blockchain Solution to Financing Infrastructure in Emerging Markets and Developing Economies. *ADB-IGF Special Working Paper Series: Fintech to Enable Development, Investment, Financial Inclusion, and Sustainability.* https://papers.ssrn.com/sol3/papers.cfm?abstract_id=3837703.

be especially beneficial in developing economies, which face greater constraints to financing infrastructure. For example, tokenization could boost private sector confidence and enthusiasm by improving infrastructure asset liquidity, opening access to small-scale projects, expanding the investor pool, mitigating cross-border currency risks impacting the bankability of projects, and reducing counterparty risks. From the perspective of governments, tokenization can improve administrative and financial efficiencies through automated auditing, enhanced project monitoring, and lowering costs.

As an emerging solution, some major challenges currently constrain the potential of asset tokenization in most economies. Tian et al. (2020) explains that regulatory uncertainty—for example, in difficulties with determining asset classes and reporting structures—is among the most significant, especially for emerging economies. Another major challenge is guaranteeing the connection between the token and the asset. To achieve this, an independent entity must act as a trusted central party to ensure that tokens are backed by the underlying infrastructure assets.

### Blockchain-based Project Bonds

Traditionally, many economies have prioritized strategies, such as blended finance solutions, which aim to attract more international capital to meet investment needs. However, so far their success has been limited (Attridge and Eigen 2019) and critics have pointed out that they can introduce financial stability risks for emerging economies. Instead, Chen and Volz (2021) argue that to drive development in emerging economies, greater focus should be applied to mobilizing domestic resources.

An emerging opportunity to achieve this is the use of blockchain-based project bonds to mobilize domestic savings to finance sustainable investments.[10] As highlighted in Case Study 7 (below), the M-Akiba retail bond pilot program in Kenya is a useful example of how technology can help governments create a more inclusive investment landscape. Chen and Volz (2021) outline the potential of a digital crowdfunding platform using the blockchain to "transparently record and certify the use of proceeds, sustainability impact and revenue streams of the project" (p. 13). Key advantages of the approach include enabling more investors to purchase "safe" local-currency assets, increasing project management efficiencies through easy technical solutions for metering and billing, and creating full transparency across the life cycle of the investment.

---

[10]    For further information on blockchain-based project bonds: Y. Chen and U. Volz. 2021. Scaling Up Sustainable Investment through Blockchain-Based Project Bonds. *Development Policy Review*. https://onlinelibrary.wiley. com/doi/epdf/10.1111/dpr.12582 (accessed 6 August 2021).

### Case Study 7: Government of Kenya's M-Akiba Bond

The Government of Kenya has been a strong supporter in the development of its local mobile banking ecosystem. In 2017, the government issued the first M-Akiba (M-Savings in Swahili) bond as a pilot. This bond, which was created to finance infrastructure projects, was innovative given that its core focus was on offering accessibility to a much broader portion of domestic investors and democratizing access to capital markets products.

With over 27 million mobile phone users and a strong mobile money user base through the M-Pesa mobile wallet, which was launched in 2007, the M-Akiba bond provided an opportunity for the government to access new domestic capital. The M-Akiba bond could be purchased exclusively by phone and offered 10% annual interest and a tenor of 3 years. To make it as accessible to the general public as possible, the minimum purchase amount was only $30, far lower than the minimum $490 investment for previous government bonds (Kazeem 2018).

While the bond failed to meet its investment target, raising $2.47 million against a target of $10 million, a key element of success was the fact that 85% of customers had never purchased a bond before (FSD Africa 2018). Issues hindering uptake were identified. They included problems with timing, communications, and customer service. However, the success in attracting so many new investors has made M-Akiba an important example of the possibilities enabled by such technology-supported bonds to broaden the investor base and help meet growing infrastructure investment needs.

Source: U. Volz. 2021. The Emergence of Innovative Financing Mechanisms to Bridge the Digital Infrastructure Investment Gap. Presentation at the 2021 Asia-Pacific Financial Inclusion Forum. 25 May. https://drive.google.com/file/d/1-scP1SthJIRzk3fjPXlZ LhYQDAMYVXn_/view (accessed 15 November 2021).

## Crowdfunding

Crowdfunding collects small amounts of capital from a large number of individuals to finance a business, project, or other investment need.[11] By utilizing social media or specialized digital platforms, crowdfunding connects entrepreneurs with a wider pool of investors (Smith 2021). Emerging in the wake of the 2008 global financial crisis, when many early-stage enterprises, entrepreneurs, or artisans had significant difficulty raising funds, crowdfunding has since grown increasingly popular for raising money, particularly in developed economies (Best et al. 2013).

In a study of crowdfunding for infrastructure projects, Pranata et al. (2020) noted that while used mostly to fund creative projects or to address social issues, crowdfunding has been used to successfully finance infrastructure projects in a growing number of cases in Europe and North America. Based on these examples and the general rise in fintech development in Asia, their study concludes that crowdfunding represents an emerging opportunity for governments seeking innovative solutions to narrow the investment gap.

---

[11]    A more detailed overview of crowdfunding and its potential in emerging markets can be found in N. Pranata et al. 2020. Crowdfunding for Infrastructure Project Financing: Lesson Learned for Asian Countries. Singapore: Asian Bureau of Finance and Economic Research. http://abfer.org/media/abfer -events-2020/specialty-conf/ 33_paper_Pranata_et_al_Crowdfunding-for -Infrastructure-Project-Financing.pdf (accessed 18 March 2021).

Pranata et al. (2020) explained that some key advantages of crowdfunding over traditional capital raising methods include its ability to connect a wide range of investors and projects regardless of geographic borders and minimizing risk through the use of advanced technologies. However, for crowdfunding to become a viable solution, governments across the region will need support a number of developments such as the promotion of domestic crowdfunding platforms and establishing a regional crowdfunding network to share experiences between economies and formulate cross-border crowdfunding regulation.

# 5. RECOMMENDATIONS FOR POLICY MAKERS AND REGULATORS

The role of financial inclusion in enhancing the well-being and resilience of the poorest and most vulnerable has come into greater focus during the COVID-19 pandemic. The following recommendations intend to provide guidance to policy makers and regulators on ways to utilize financial inclusion strategies effectively as a means to support those at the base of the economy, stimulate economic recovery, and prepare for emerging challenges and opportunities that result from an increasingly digitized world.

(i)    *Support the capacity of microfinance providers to adopt digital technology to drive financial inclusion and bring the benefits of the digital economy to their clients.*

Digital transformation could increase income and wealth inequality by widening the digital divide between those who have access to, and are capable of using, digital technology and those without. Traditionally, microfinance providers have played an important role in providing financial services to those at the base of the economy, including informal sector workers and MSMEs. By leveraging the reach and degree of trust they often enjoy with their clients, microfinance providers can adopt digital technology to improve both operations and the services they offer to clients, particularly during the COVID-19 pandemic. Specific actions governments might take to facilitate this include:

- **Promote and ensure equitable access to digital infrastructure.** Steps need to be taken to close the digital divide for everyone in the ecosystem and expand investment in digital infrastructure. For example, data connectivity remains a significant challenge across the region, especially in rural areas where many microfinance providers operate. Furthermore, domestic payment systems often have limited use among nonbank financial institutions, including many microfinance providers. In this respect, interoperability and reach are key. Enabling access with appropriate risk mitigation measures can provide a more competitive environment, facilitate interoperability, and enable greater efficiencies.

- **Develop and promote a fully functioning digital identity system.** Digital financial services are strongly anchored to the need for digital identity. A lack of formal identification limits participation in the digital economy. If designed and implemented properly, digital identification (both for individuals and corporates) can unlock economic value, close financial inclusion gaps, and minimize risks such as fraud and over-indebtedness. It can further help microfinance providers and intermediaries carry out customer due diligence efficiently, reducing the cost of customer acquisition, which not only supports inclusion but also innovation and competition.

- **Develop enabling policy and enhance regulation for new technologies in close coordination with other government agencies that also support innovation and technology.** Policies and regulations on data privacy and protection, data sovereignty, digital identity, harmonized wallet and prepaid SIM registration or cybersecurity all enable digital finance technologies. However, they do not necessarily fall neatly under the remit of the financial regulator.

**(ii)    *Prioritize investments in open digital ecosystems that accelerates digitization of payments leading to inclusive recovery, resilience, and financial inclusion.***

Financial inclusion priorities should focus on solutions for providing immediate relief (i.e., digital social payments) that can open up choices and ease of access for the poor, creating opportunity—such as from income generation—to support growth and build resilience against future shocks. To develop a secure and competitive digital financial ecosystem, governments can consider a range of aspects. These include data privacy, cybersecurity, digital identification, fair competition, physical infrastructure, connectivity, interoperability, and financial and digital literacy. Due to the sheer volume of cash transfers passing through the growing digital payments infrastructure, getting it right for everyone is an important task for governments. While areas of data privacy, digital governance, and consent frameworks are nascent and complex, they are essential for building trust and adoption leading to greater financial inclusion. Specific actions governments might take to achieve this include:

- **Support the development of responsible digital ecosystems.** Governments and their regulatory authorities can invest in platform design, architecture, and technical support to play a significant role in framing the development of digital ecosystems in their economy. Due to the ongoing impact of COVID-19, particular importance should be placed on expediting regulatory measures that reduce systemic exclusion of the most vulnerable from access to and usage of a range of financial services, including support for increasing digital financial literacy.

- **Facilitate the creation and implementation of good governance.** Governments should take a proactive regulatory approach to address new risks and the amplification of existing risks (i.e., potential for more fraud incidents), arising from increased digital financial transfers adoption. This can include establishing, and providing adequate supervision for, appropriate technology rules and processes that mitigate potential risks (i.e., legislation that encapsulates consumer protection frameworks such as cybersecurity and data protection laws).

- **Support the growth of a vibrant technology community.** This should include open-source technology start-ups and civil-society stakeholders, which are important stewards of user experiences.

**(iii)   *Support innovation as part of COVID-19 recovery strategies.***

COVID-19 has highlighted the significant role of digital finance in building resilience in a crisis. However, in many ways, the use of digital technology to support resilience among the poor has been less successful where economies lack key enablers such as robust digital identity schemes, widespread account access, and interoperable payment systems. For digital technology to meaningfully support the region's most vulnerable populations, greater innovation is needed to develop new approaches and business models. Actions governments can take to establish a foundation for this include:

- **Build the infrastructure of digital finance.** This should be based upon ensuring digital access (i.e., mobile or internet) to as much of the population as possible. From this foundation, governments should focus on achieving the needed combination of sovereign digital identification, simplified account opening and systems to be able to use networked Golden Source data (i.e., digitization of definitive or official data sources) enabled with open access and interoperable payments systems. The combination of these elements is essential and forms an ecosystem that provides for other important developments including digitization of government payments or services (which has been crucial during the COVID-19 pandemic).

- **Design appropriate regulatory approaches.** These approaches should be risk-based, tiered, and proportional to ensure that as risk increases, so too does relevant regulation and supervision. The use of technology can also provide important means to increase regulation and supervision efficiency. Regulatory technologies, or "Regtech," can facilitate meeting monitoring, reporting, and compliance requirements effectively and efficiently, while "Suptech" relates to how supervisors leverage technological advancements, e.g., through digitization of data or the automation of reporting and data collection by supervisors.

- **Provide support for the wider data ecosystem.** Core to this is a framework around how data are collected and used. As digital transformation accelerates, it is becoming of greater importance to governments how to build frameworks that will enable the most effective use of data across society to support development while minimizing associated risks. To address this, governments should provide direct support to needed research and development including establishing innovation hubs and regulatory sandboxes.

**(iv)   *Reassess financial inclusion strategies to consider the growing use of digital financial services.***

The fast-moving pace of technology and fintech developments, including new innovative digital products and services entering the market, continues to accelerate because of the COVID-19 pandemic. While studies have shown that higher financial inclusion positively impact aspects such as poverty, income inequality, women's empowerment or entrepreneurship, increased use of technology in financial markets is rapidly changing the financial inclusion landscape. To ensure that financial inclusion strategies have the greatest impact on socioeconomic outcomes, governments need to reassess their strategies and continue to align them with an increasingly digital world. Specific examples of actions governments can take to achieve this include:

- **Build a digital transformation roadmap within the context of financial inclusion.** As the growth and development of digital financial services continues to expand, alignment between financial inclusion and digital transformation strategies will become more important. Such alignment will help ensure that concrete actions can be implemented consistently and promote greater collaboration among a wider set of stakeholders to achieve scale.

- **Consider new dimensions of financial inclusion.** Financial inclusion is a complex phenomenon linked to many underlying factors and evolving conditions. Besides traditional supply (access) and demand (usage) dimensions, fintech infrastructure and financial development (i.e., ease of getting credit, bank concentration, financial system deposits to GDP, and depth of credit information) should be considered as they also contribute to financial inclusion.

- **Recognize that the impact of financial inclusion varies depending on the economy's state of development.** The varying significance and impacts of financial inclusion and its multiple dimensions across income groups suggest that economy characteristics, including income levels, need to be considered in developing effective policies to promote financial inclusion as part of economy-wide development strategies.

- **Prioritize financial inclusion policies that will have a greater effect on socioeconomic outcomes.** The impact of financial inclusion and its dimensions (i.e., access, usage, financial development, and fintech infrastructure) is not universal across economies. Some aspects of financial inclusion may be more important than others in achieving positive socioeconomic outcomes depending on economy-specific situations proxied by different income levels. When assessing these priorities, governments should pay adequate attention to demand-side factors. For example, digital finance literacy programs targeting all sectors can be important for improving trust and confidence in the digital finance ecosystem and drive usage and impact.

(v)    *Take steps to promote greater stakeholder cooperation to progress digital financial inclusion at the base of the economy.*

While the fintech sector continues to expand due to the COVID-19 pandemic, most financial institutions are still unable to serve their customers digitally; particularly at the lower ends of the market where many people remain financially excluded. Furthermore, very few fintechs or traditional financial institutions are focused on providing digital services to the lower ends of the market despite significant potential for business growth opportunities due to persistent challenges such as illiteracy, reliance on cash, lack of digital financial literacy or limited access to digital infrastructure. As the usability of technology continuously improves, governments can support cooperation between fintechs and financial institutions to enable more people at the base of the economy to receive digital services. Some specific actions governments may consider to encourage this include:

- **Reimagine regulatory technology risk management frameworks.** Many frameworks currently in use are based on older technology that was more complex and difficult to integrate than what is used today. Appropriate processes should be adopted, promoting more efficient de-risking of digital transformation by bringing together multiple fintechs to support rapid digital product prototyping and identifying those that meet needs most effectively.

- **Fast-track regulatory licensing process for microfinance providers going digital.** An important aspect would be for regulators to recognize existing frameworks that microfinance providers might leverage rather than treating each digital journey as a unique case. Furthermore, governments can provide standard, open application program interfaces (APIs) to streamline regulatory reporting requirements.

- **Establish legislation with clear timelines for fully open banking APIs for domestic incumbent players.** For example, national or international payment gateways, tier-1 banks, credit bureaus, and the like are not often able to acquire API definitions easily. Publishing all APIs as open source will support greater integration and connectivity in the financial ecosystem. This will help level the playing field for smaller microfinance providers and local and/or global fintechs and accelerate digital transformation. Since the enactment of legislation is often a long process, governments might consider the adoption of an economy-wide framework in the short term.

**(vi)** *Explore the potential of innovative fintech financing mechanisms for digital infrastructure development needs.*

Closing the financing gaps for digital infrastructure development is a significant challenge for many governments, especially developing economies with less developed capital markets. However, addressing these gaps and enabling the development of safe, reliable, and affordable digital infrastructure is critical to achieving digital financial inclusion. As technology continues to develop at a rapid pace, emerging fintech models such as asset tokenization, blockchain-based project bonds, or crowdfunding provide potential innovative solutions for raising capital. Specific actions governments could take to explore and enable these innovations further include:

- **Identify and invest in key digital systems.** To harness the potential of innovative fintech solutions to help generate investment capital, certain digital systems such as crowdfunding platforms, mobile banking or tokenization of debt/equity instruments need to be in place. Governments should consider priorities for enabling fintech to develop viable solutions for mobilizing domestic savings and scaling up sustainable investment opportunities.

- **Nurture talent to enhance internal capabilities.** This might include placement of technology experts within central banks or other government ministries as well as establishing a dedicated core technology innovation group or an expert network to provide several functions such as identifying potential innovative models and use cases, facilitating public-private collaboration, or coordination with international partners.

- **Explore different innovative fintech solutions to mobilize domestic savings.** To fill the digital infrastructure financing gap, financial authorities should take a proactive approach to identifying which fintech solutions may be most effective in facilitating domestic resource mobilization and contribute to financial inclusion. Furthermore, they also need to create adequate regulatory frameworks that allow promising fintech solutions to be developed while safeguarding financial stability and consumer protection. The most appropriate solutions will vary between economies dependent on local circumstances. Greater international cooperation to share lessons and best practice would support efforts.

# REFERENCES

Agarwal, S. 2019. 95% of People Have Aadhaar and Use it Once a Month on Average: Report. *ETGovernment.* https://government.economictimes.indiatimes.com/news/digital-india/95-of-people-have-aadhaar-and-use-it-once-a-month-on-average-report/72236213 (accessed 4 March 2021).

Arner, D. W., R. P. Buckley, and D. A. Zetzsche. 2018. Fintech for Financial Inclusion: A Framework for Digital Financial Transformation. *UNSW Law Research Paper. No. 18-87. University of Hong Kong Faculty of Law Research Paper No. 2019/001, University of Luxembourg Law Working Paper. No. 004-2019.* https://papers.ssrn.com/sol3/papers.cfm?abstract_id=3245287 (accessed 2 June 2021).

Asian Development Bank (ADB). 2018. *Harnessing Technology for More Inclusive and Sustainable Finance in Asia and the Pacific.* Manila. https://www.adb.org/sites/default/files/publication/456936/technology-finance-asia-pacific.pdf (accessed 3 March 2021).

———. 2021a. *Asian Economic Integration Report 2021: Making Digital Platforms Work for Asia and the Pacific.* Manila.

———. 2021b. *Asian Development Outlook 2021: Financing Green and Inclusive Recovery.* Manila. https://www.adb.org/sites/default/files/publication/692111/ado2021.pdf (accessed 2 June 2021).

———. 2021c. ADB COVID-19 Policy Database. https://covid19policy.adb.org/ (accessed 24 July 2021).

———. 2021d. *Fintech to Enable Development, Investment, Financial Inclusion, and Sustainability. Conference Highlights.* Manila. https://www.adb.org/sites/default/files/publication/704236/fintech-development-conference-highlights.pdf (accessed 2 June 2021).

Asian Infrastructure Investment Bank (AIIB). 2020a. *Digital Infrastructure Sector Strategy: AIIB's Role in the Growth of the Digital Economy of the 21st Century.* Beijing. https://www.aiib.org/en/policies-strategies/operational-policies/digital-infrastructure-strategy/.content/_download/AIIB-Digital-Strategy.pdf (accessed 15 March 2021).

——. 2020b. Digital Infrastructure Sector Analysis. Market Analysis and Technical Studies. https://www.aiib.org/en/policies-strategies/operational-policies/digital-infrastructure-strategy/.content/_download/Full-DISA-Report_final-with-Appendix-2020-01-10.pdf (accessed 15 March 2021).

Asia-Pacific Economic Cooperation (APEC). 2020. The 27th APEC Economic Leaders' Meeting, 2020 Kuala Lumpur Declaration. Singapore. https://www.apec.org/Meeting-Papers/Leaders-Declarations/2020/2020_aelm (accessed 20 February 2021).

——. 2021. APEC Putrajaya Vision 2040. Singapore. https://www.apec.org/Meeting-Papers/Leaders-Declarations/2020/2020_aelm/Annex-A (accessed 24 July 2021).

Attridge, S. and L. Eigen. 2019. Blended Finance in the Poorest Countries: The Need for a Better Approach. London: Overseas Development Institute.

Banchongduang, S. 2021. PromptPay Linked to Singapore's PayNow. Bangkok Post. 30 April. https://www.bangkokpost.com/business/2108119/promptpay-linked-to-singapores-paynow (accessed 24 July 2021).

Bangko Sentral ng Pilipinas (BSP). 2020. Financial Stability Report: 2nd Semester 2020. Manila. https://www.bsp.gov.ph/Media_And_Research/FSR/FSR2020_2NDSEM.pdf (accessed 24 July 2021).

——. 2021. Payments and Settlements—National Retail Payment System. Manila. https://www.bsp.gov.ph/Pages/PAYMENTS%20AND%20SETTLEMENTS_deletethis/National%20Retail%20Payment%20System/National-Retail-Payment-System.aspx (accessed 24 July 2021).

Bangkok Post. 2020. Cash Handouts for Informal Workers. 25 March. https://www.bangkokpost.com/thailand/general/1885640/cash-handouts-for-informal-workers (accessed 24 July 2021).

Beck, T. 2020. Fintech and Financial Inclusion: Opportunities and Pitfalls. Tokyo: Asian Development Bank Institute. https://www.adb.org/sites/default/files/publication/623276/adbi-wp1165.pdf (accessed 6 March 2021).

Begazo, T. 2020. COVID-19: We're Tracking Digital Responses Worldwide. Here's What We See. World Bank Blog. 5 May. https://blogs.worldbank.org/digital-development/covid-19-were-tracking-digital-responses-worldwide-heres-what-we-see (accessed 22 February 2021).

Benni, N. 2021. Digital Finance and Inclusion in the Time of COVID-19: Lessons, Experiences and Proposals. Rome: Food and Agriculture Organization of the United Nations. http://www.fao.org/3/cb2109en/CB2109EN.pdf (accessed 10 March 2021).

Best, J. et al. 2013. *Crowdfunding's Potential for the Developing World. InfoDev.* Washington, DC: World Bank. http://documents.worldbank.org/curated/en/409841468327411701/Crowdfundings-potential-for-the-developing-world (accessed 18 March 2021).

Better Than Cash Alliance (BTCA). 2016. *Responsible Digital Payments Guidelines.* https://btca-production-site.s3.amazonaws.com/documents/212/english _attachments/DigitalGuidelines-withMemo-MECH-Update1d.pdf?15047 14863 (accessed 3 March 2021).

Bhardwaj, M., Y. Hedrick-Wong, and H. Thomas. Financial Inclusion for Asia's Unbanked. *World Bank Blogs.* 30 April. https://blogs.worldbank.org/allaboutfinance/financial-inclusion-asias-unbanked (accessed 2 August 2021).

Bull, G. 2020. After the Storm: How Microfinance Can Adapt and Thrive. *The Consultative Group to Assist the Poor Blog.* https://www.cgap.org/blog/after -storm-how-microfinance-can-adapt-and-thrive (accessed 2 March 2021).

——. 2018. 6 Ways Microfinance Institutions Can Adapt to the Digital Age. *The Consultative Group to Assist the Poor Blog.* https://www.cgap.org/blog/6-ways -microfinance-institutions-can-adapt-digital-age (accessed 5 March 2021).

CB Insights. 2020. *The State Of Fintech Q1 '20 Report: Investment and the Sector Trends to Watch.* New York. https://www.cbinsights.com/research/report/fintech -trends-q4-2020/ (accessed 8 March 2020).

Chen, Y. and U. Volz. 2021. Scaling Up Sustainable Investment through Blockchain-based Project Bonds. *Development Policy Review.* https://online library.wiley.com/doi/10.1111/dpr.12582 (accessed 6 August 2021).

*Council of European Professional Informatics Societies* (CEPIS). 2020. Commission President Commits to Invest 20% of NextGenerationEU in Digital. https://cepis. org/commission-president-commits-to-invest-20-of-nextgenerationeu-in -digital/ (accessed 22 February 2021).

Crisanto, J. M. 2021. Indonesia E-wallet Transaction to Reach $18.5 Billion in 2021 Amid Fierce Competition. *The Asian Banker.* 9 April. https://www.theasian banker.com/updates-and-articles/big-tech-platforms-heat-up-competition -in-indonesias-digital-payments-landscape (accessed 2 June 2021).

Dash, S. 2020. Digitisation is the Only Choice for Small Businesses in India—and It May Add Up to $200 Billion to the GDP. *Business Insider India.* 31 July. https://www.businessinsider.in/business/news/digitisation-is-the-only-choice -for-small-businesses-in-india-and-it-may-add-up-to-200-billion-to-the -gdp/articleshow/77215217.cms (accessed 20 February 2021).

Davidovic, S., D. Prady, and H. Tourpe. 2020. You've Got Money: Mobile Payments Help People During the Pandemic. International Monetary Fund. *IMFBlog*, 22 June. https://blogs.imf.org/2020/06/22/youve-got-money-mobile-pay ments-help-people-during-the-pandemic/ (accessed 20 February 2021).

*Deloitte*. 2020. Beyond COVID-19: New Opportunities for Fintech Companies. https://www2.deloitte.com/us/en/pages/financial-services/articles/beyond -covid-19-new-opportunities-for-fintech-companies.html (accessed 8 March 2021).

Demirgüç-Kunt, A. et al. 2018. *The Global Findex Database 2017: Measuring Financial Inclusion and the Fintech Revolution*. Washington, DC: World Bank.

D'Silva, D. et al. 2019. The Design of Digital Financial Infrastructure: Lessons from India. *BIS Papers. No. 106*. Basel: Bank for International Settlements. https://www.bis.org/publ/bppdf/bispap106.pdf (accessed 7 March 2021).

Economic and Social Commission for Asia and the Pacific (ESCAP). 2018. *Inequality in Asia and the Pacific in the Era of the 2030 Agenda for Sustainable Development*. New York: United Nations. https://www.unescap.org/publications/inequality -asia-and-pacific-era-2030-agenda-sustainable-development (accessed 23 February 2021).

European Commission. 2020. Recovery Plan for Europe. Brussels. https://ec.europa. eu/info/strategy/recovery-plan-europe_en (accessed 22 February 2021).

Fakhoury, I. 2020. How the World Bank is Looking at COVID-19 and Public-Private Partnerships, Right Now and Post-Crisis. *World Bank Blog*. 10 June. https://blogs.worldbank.org/ppps/how-world-bank-looking-covid-19-and-public -private-partnerships-right-now-and-post-crisis (accessed 8 March 2021).

Franken, P. 2021. The Evolving Fintech Landscape and the Role of Stakeholder Cooperation to Progress Digital Financial Inclusion at the Base of the Economy. Presentation at the 2021 Asia-Pacific Financial Inclusion Forum. 25 May. https://drive.google.com/file/d/18RKV2Yng-tF1uU0HILNC14fRrtKPQW63/ view (accessed 12 June 2021).

Financial Sector Deepening Africa (FSDA). 2018. *M-Akiba Post Issuance Survey*. Nairobi. https://www.fsdafrica.org/wp-content/uploads/2019/08/18-06-20-M -Akiba-Post-Issuance-Survey.pdf (accessed 2 June 2021).

Gaylican, C. 2021. Mobile Payment Apps Pave the Road to Financial Inclusion. *The Manila Times*. 30 March. https://www.manilatimes.net/2021/03/30/supple ments/mobile-payment-apps-pave-the-road-to-financial-inclusion/857147/ (accessed 2 June 2021).

Gentilini, U., M. Almenfi, and P. Dale. 2020. Social Protection and Jobs Responses to COVID-19: A Real-Time Review of Country Measures. *COVID-19 Living Paper*. Washington, DC: World Bank Group. https://documents.worldbank.org/en/publication/documents-reports/documentdetail/467521607723220511/pdf (accessed 1 September 2021).

Global System for Mobile Communications Association (GSMA). 2020. *Advancing Digital Societies in Asia Pacific: A Whole-of-Government Approach.* https://www.gsma.com/asia-pacific/wp-content/uploads/2020/11/201031-Digi Soc.pdf (accessed 24 July 2021).

Gopinath, G. 2020. A Long, Uneven and Uncertain Ascent. *IMFBlog*. https://blogs.imf.org/2020/10/13/a-long-uneven-and-uncertain-ascent/ (accessed 27 February 2021).

Hernandez, E. 2020. Financial Inclusion for What? *Consultative Group to Assist the Poor Blog. 5 February.* https://www.cgap.org/blog/financial-inclusion-what (accessed 28 February 2021).

Hunter, S. and S. Taylor. 2020. *Enabling Shared Prosperity Through Inclusive Finance: Leaving No One Behind in an Age of Disruption.* Kenmore, Australia: The Foundation for Development Cooperation. https://www2.abaconline.org/assets/2020_APFIF_FINAL_REPORT_1.pdf (accessed 28 February 2021).

International Monetary Fund (IMF). 2020. *Fiscal Monitor: Policies for the Recovery.* Washington, DC. https://www.imf.org/en/Publications/FM/Issues/2020/09/30/october-2020-fiscal-monitor#Full%20Report%20and%20Executive%20 Summary (accessed 3 March 2021).

Jurzyk, E. et al. 2020. *COVID-19 and Inequality in Asia: Breaking the Vicious Cycle.* Washington, DC: International Monetary Fund. https://www.imf.org/en/Publications/WP/Issues/2020/10/16/COVID-19-and-Inequality-in-Asia-Breaking-the-Vicious-Cycle-49807 (accessed 23 February 2021).

Kazeem, Y. 2018. The World's First Mobile-Only Government Bond in Kenya Is Popular, but Missed Its Target. *Quartz Africa.* 21 June. https://qz.com/africa/1310232/kenyas-m-akiba-mobile-money-bond-is-popular-but-misses-target/ (accessed 2 June 2021).

Kharas, H. 2020. The Impact of COVID-19 on Global Extreme Poverty. *Brookings.* 21 October. https://www.brookings.edu/blog/future-development/2020/10/21/the-impact-of-covid-19-on-global-extreme-poverty/ (accessed 27 February 2021).

Khera, P. et al. 2021. Measuring Digital Financial Inclusion in Emerging Market and Developing Economies: A New Index. *IMF Working Paper. No. 21/90.* Washington, DC: International Monetary Fund.

Kirton, J. 2020. From Response to Recovery: How the COVID-19 Crisis Will Accelerate Digitization in Microfinance. *FINCA Ventures.* https://fincaventures.com/from-response-to-recovery-how-the-covid-19-crisis-will-accelerate -digitization-in-microfinance/ (accessed 3 March 2021).

Lakner, C. et al. 2021. Updated Estimates of the Impact of COVID-19 on Global Poverty: Looking Back at 2020 and the Outlook for 2021. *World Bank Blog. 11 January.* https://blogs.worldbank.org/opendata/updated-estimates-impact -covid-19-global-poverty-looking-back-2020-and-outlook-2021 (accessed 28 February 2021).

Le Moral, L. 2020. What's Next for Fintech? Moving Forward with Lessons Learned From This Pandemic. In *The Post-COVID-19 Financial System: Global Future Council on Financial and Monetary Systems.* Geneva: World Economic Forum. http://www3.weforum.org/docs/WEF_GFC_Bookend_Endnotes_Report _2020.pdf (accessed 5 March 2021).

Lucas, D. 2021. Digital Payments Surged by over 5,000 Percent amid Pandemic, says BSP Chief. *Inquirer.Net.* 4 February. https://business.inquirer.net/316989/digital -payments-surged-by-over-5000-percent-amid-pandemic-says-bsp-chief (accessed 24 July 2021).

MacArthur, H. et al. 2020. Implications for Fintech and Payments Private Equity Investors. Bain & Company Webinar. 19 May. https://www.bain.com/insights/ implications-fintech-payments-private-equity-investors-webinar/ (accessed 3 March 2021).

Magats, J. 2020. How Partnership, Collaboration and Access to Technology Can Help Speed Recovery. In *The Post-COVID-19 Financial System: Global Future Council on Financial and Monetary Systems.* Geneva: World Economic Forum. http://www3.weforum.org/docs/WEF_GFC_Bookend_Endnotes_Report _2020.pdf (accessed 5 March 2021).

*McKinsey and Company.* 2020. How COVID-19 Has Pushed Companies Over the Technology Tipping Point—and Transformed Business Forever. https://www.mckinsey.com/business-functions/strategy-and-corporate-finance/ our-insights/how-covid-19-has-pushed-companies-over-the-technology-tipp ing-point-and-transformed-business-forever (accessed 20 February 2021).

McKinsey Global Institute. 2019. Infographic: What is Good Digital ID? https://www.mckinsey.com/business-functions/mckinsey-digital/our-insights/ infographic-what-is-good-digital-id (accessed 3 March 2021).

Nilekani, N. 2018. Giving People Control Over Their Data Can Transform Development. *World Bank Blog.* 11 October. https://blogs.worldbank.org/voices/ giving-people-control-over-their-data-can-transform-development (accessed 4 March 2021).

Organisation for Economic Co-operation and Development (OECD). 2020a. *Digital Disruption in Banking and Its Impact on Competition*. Paris. http://www.oecd.org/daf/competition/digital-disruption-in-banking-and-its-impact-on-competition-2020.pdf (accessed 10 March 2021).

——. 2020b. The Tokenisation of Assets and Potential Implications for Financial Markets. *OECD Blockchain Policy Series*. Paris. https://www.oecd.org/finance/The-Tokenisation-of-Assets-and-Potential-Implications-for-Financial-Markets.htm (accessed 16 March 2021).

Paine, J. 2021. Digitalisation Will Spur Post-Pandemic Recovery. *Bangkok Post*. 19 January. https://www.bangkokpost.com/opinion/opinion/2053291/digitalisation-will-spur-post-pandemic-recovery (accessed 22 February 2021).

Pangestu, M. E. 2020. Harnessing the Power of Digital ID. *World Bank Blog*. https://blogs.worldbank.org/voices/harnessing-power-digital-id (accessed 4 March 2021).

Park, C. and R. Mercado. 2021. *Understanding Financial Inclusion: What Matters and How it Matters*. ADBI Working Paper Series. No. 1287. Tokyo: Asian Development Bank Institute. https://www.adb.org/publications/understanding-financial-inclusion-what-matters-and-how-it-matters.

Pranata, N. et al. 2020. *Crowdfunding for Infrastructure Project Financing: Lessons Learned for Asian Countries*. Singapore: Asian Bureau of Finance and Economic Research. http://abfer.org/media/abfer-events-2020/specialty-conf/33_paper_Pranata_et_al_Crowdfunding-for-Infrastructure-Project-Financing.pdf (accessed 18 March 2021).

Ruddenklau, A. 2020. *Can Fintech Lead Innovation Post COVID-19? Amstelveen, Netherlands: KPMG*. https://home.kpmg/xx/en/blogs/home/posts/2020/05/can-fintech-lead-innovation-post-covid-19.html (accessed 10 March 2021).

Rutkowski, M. et al. 2020. Responding to Crisis with Digital Payments for Social Protection: Short-term Measures with Long-term Benefits. *World Bank Blog*. 31 March. https://blogs.worldbank.org/voices/responding-crisis-digital-payments-social-protection-short-term-measures-long-term-benefits (accessed 22 February 2021).

Sahay, R. et al. 2020. *The Promise of Fintech: Financial Inclusion in the Post COVID-19 Era*. Washington, DC: International Monetary Fund. https://www.imf.org/en/Publications/Departmental-Papers-Policy-Papers/Issues/2020/06/29/The-Promise-of-Fintech-Financial-Inclusion-in-the-Post-COVID-19-Era-48623 (accessed 8 March 2021).

Smith, T. 2021. Crowdfunding. *Investopia*. https://www.investopedia.com/terms/c/crowdfunding.asp (accessed 18 March 2021).

Spataro, J. 2020. *2 Years of Digital Transformation in 2 Months. Microsoft.* https://www.microsoft.com/en-us/microsoft-365/blog/2020/04/30/2-years -digital-transformation-2-months/ (accessed 20 February 2021).

Strangio, S. 2021. COVID-19 Drives Uptake of Digital Payment Systems. *The Diplomat.* 10 May. https://thediplomat.com/2021/05/covid-19-drives-uptake-of-digital -payment-systems/ (accessed 24 July 2021).

Tian, Y. et al. Asset Tokenization: A Blockchain Solution to Financing Infrastructure in Emerging Markets and Developing Economies. *ADB-IGF Special Working Paper Series: Fintech to Enable Development, Investment, Financial Inclusion, and Sustainability.* https://www.researchgate.net/publication/344672498_Asset _Tokenization_A_Blockchain_Solution_to_Financing_Infrastructure_in _Emerging_Markets_and_Developing_Economies (accessed 16 March 2021).

United Nations Department of Economic and Social Affairs (UNDESA). 2020. *United Nations E-Government Survey 2020: Digital Government in the Decade of Action for Sustainable Development.* New York. https://publicadministration.un.org/ egovkb/Portals/egovkb/Documents/un/2020-Survey/2020%20UN%20E-Gov ernment%20Survey%20(Full%20Report).pdf (accessed 20 February 2021).

UNSGSA FinTech Working Group and CCAF. 2019. *Early Lessons on Regulatory Innovations to Enable Inclusive FinTech: Innovation Offices, Regulatory Sandboxes, and RegTech.* New York and Cambridge, UK: Office of the United Nations Secretary-General's Special Advocate and Cambridge Centre for Alternative Finance.

White, O. et al. 2019. *Digital Identification: A Key to Inclusive Growth. McKinsey Global Institute.* https://www.mckinsey.com/business-functions/mckinsey-digital/ our-insights/digital-identification-a-key-to-inclusive-growth (accessed 4 March 2021).

White, O. et al. 2021. *COVID-19: Making the Case for Robust Digital Financial Infrastructure. McKinsey and Company.* https://www.mckinsey.com/industries/ financial-services/our-insights/covid-19-making-the-case-for-robust-digital -financial-infrastructure (accessed 2 March 2021).

World Bank. 2020a. Projected Poverty Impacts of COVID-19 (coronavirus). Washington, DC. https://www.worldbank.org/en/topic/poverty/brief/projected -poverty-impacts-of-COVID-19 (accessed 21 February 2021).

——. 2020b. Fintech Market Reports Rapid Growth During COVID-19 Pandemic. 3 December. https://www.worldbank.org/en/news/press-release/2020/12/03/ fintech-market-reports-rapid-growth-during-covid-19-pandemic (accessed 2 March 2021).

——. 2021. World Development Indicators. https://databank.worldbank.org/home. aspx (accessed 26 July 2021).

World Economic Forum. 2018. *Financing a Forward-Looking Internet for All*. Geneva. http://www3.weforum.org/docs/WP_Financing_Forward-Looking_Internet _for_All_report_2018.pdf (accessed 24 July 2021).

———. 2020. *Accelerating Digital Inclusion in the New Normal*. Geneva. http://www3. weforum.org/docs/WEF_Accelerating_Digital_Inclusion_in_the_New _Normal_Report_2020.pdf (accessed 23 February 2021).

Xiao, Y. and K. N. Massally. 2021. 7 Lessons COVID-19 Taught Us About Improving Digital Payments. *World Economic Forum*. 13 January. https://www.weforum.org/ agenda/2021/01/davos-agenda-digital-payments-7-lessons-covid-19-taught -us/ (accessed 3 March 2021).

Xiao, Y. and M. Chorzempa. 2020. How Digital Payments Can Help Countries Cope with COVID-19, Other Pandemics: Lessons from China. *World Economic Forum*. 6 May. https://www.weforum.org/agenda/2020/05/digital-payments-cash-and -covid-19-pandemics/ (accessed 20 February 2021).

Zetzsche, D. A. et al. 2020. *Fintech Toolkit: Smart Regulatory and Market Approaches to Financial Technology Innovation*. Bonn: Deutsche Gesellschaft für Internationale Zusammenarbeit (GIZ). https://papers.ssrn.com/sol3/papers.cfm?abstract_id =3598142 (accessed 7 March 2021).

www.ingramcontent.com/pod-product-compliance
Lightning Source LLC
Chambersburg PA
CBHW050052220326

41599CB00045B/7379